The History of the Kingdom of God

Part I

From Creation to Parousia

The History of the Kingdom of God

Part I

From Creation to Parousia

Sofia Cavalletti

Translated from the Italian by Rebekah Rojcewicz

Catechesis of
the Good Shepherd
Publications

Nihil Obstat
Very Reverend Daniel A. Smilanic, JCD
Vicar for Canonical Services
Archdiocese of Chicago
December 7, 2011

Imprimatur
Reverend John F. Canary, STL, DMIN
Vicar General
Archdiocese of Chicago
December 7, 2011

The *Nihil Obstat* and *Imprimatur* are official declarations that the material is free
from doctrinal or moral error, and thus is granted permission to publish in
accordance with c. 827. No legal responsibility is assumed by the grant of
this permission. No implication is contained herein that those who have granted
the *Nihil Obstat* and *Imprimatur* agree with the content, opinions, or statements
expressed.

THE HISTORY OF THE KINGDOM OF GOD, PART 1: FROM CREATION TO PAROUSIA
(formerly History's Golden Thread) © 2012 Archdiocese of Chicago:
Liturgy Training Publications, 3949 South Racine Avenue, Chicago IL 60609;
1-800-933-1800; orders@ltp.org; fax 1-800-933-7094. All rights reserved.
See our website at www.LTP.org.

The cover illustration was done by Julie Lonneman.

Printed in the United States of America.

Library of Congress Control Number: 2011943972

16   15   14   13   12   1   2   3   4   5

ISBN 978-1-61671-048-4

HKG1

Contents

Translator's Note to History's Golden Thread

First of all, I want to thank Dr. Cavalletti for the gift of this beautiful text, as well as for the privilege of being entrusted with the long work of translating it from the Italian. I am also deeply grateful to Nicolina Gleasure for her invaluable assistance with the first draft. Finally, I want to thank the catechists of the Good Shepherd for their patience in awaiting the completion of the English translation of this primary source for working with older children on the history of salvation.

Rebekah Rojcewicz

Translator's Note to the Revised Edition

It has been a gift to work on this new edition of the first book I ever translated. That first English edition, called *History's Golden Thread* was a "long work" indeed, taking me almost ten years to complete. It was not a matter of the book being so big, but of my being so "little." I was far from being a master of the Italian language, and I was simultaneously immersed in the work and adventure of being a mother of young children, a catechist of children, and a catechist formation leader in the Catechesis of the Good Shepherd. With the generous assistance of Nicolina Gleasure (now deceased), that first edition made it to print in 1999.

For this second edition, I am especially grateful to Patricia Coulter and Margaret Brennan for their invaluable assistance in the translation and editing work. And, as ever, I am deeply grateful to Sofia Cavalletti for the immense gift of this beautiful text and the "exorbitant privilege" (Charles Peguy) of working on the translation.

What is new or different about this second English edition? I find it particularly striking that Sofia Cavalletti seems to have deleted more text than she has added. It is even more essential, and I see this as a fruit of Cavalletti's more than fifty years of patient observation of and work with children in the atrium (the prepared environment for children's faith formation in the Catechesis of the Good Shepherd). Essentiality is one of the strongest spiritual characteristics of even the youngest children, and it is also one of the most severe disciplines for most adults. In this book, the less is truly more, for it enables us to more readily detect the "golden thread," the plan of God that binds together the whole history of salvation.

The newest part of this second edition is the chapter on miracles. The chapter on miracles in the first English edition was true and beautiful—and one might think essential enough. But the new miracles chapter is even richer, truer, and more beautiful. I believe this is so because of Sofia's longtime search for the most essential way to approach the mystery of Jesus' miracles with older children. This research led to not one but two time-intensive efforts to make an appropriate material for the children's personal work. The new miracles chapter reflects the wisdom the children have brought to the table in their responses to this work.

Finally, there is the simple but very important feature of the new book title and cover which will only be fully appreciated once its companion volume has been published: *The History of the Kingdom of God, Part II: Liturgy and the Building of the Kingdom* (forthcoming). Hence, a deep current throughout Dr. Cavalletti's scholarship and also in the Catechesis of the Good Shepherd—the Bible-liturgy unity—is further "set afire."

Rebekah Rojcewicz
June 15, 2011

Introduction to the First Italian Edition

This small book is intended to offer the reader a key to the reading of the biblical text—the Old and New Testaments. It presents a method that is meant to accompany and sustain one in the reading of the text that contains the word of God—a timeless word, but one that comes to us through the cultural expressions of a specific people, the people of Israel.

It has been said that in order to understand God, it is necessary to understand Israel. Israel is a Semitic people. Although to do so is perhaps an overgeneralization, one could say that western civilizations can be defined by the way they seek the truth. This search is pursued, above all, intellectually. The "truth" that is reached in this way could then appear to be more the fruit of human speculation than a gift of God, even if this speculation is based on the consideration of creation, the point of departure in seeking knowledge of God for the Gentile (Romans 1:20; cf. Wisdom 13:9). By contrast, the people of Israel take a listening stance toward God, completely attentive to whatever God reveals of himself through history and the words of the prophets. In Israel it is not the philosopher who is great, but the prophet, the one who can say, "The Lord of hosts has sworn in my hearing . . ." (Isaiah 5:9).

This difference in attitude toward the truth is determined more by the fact that Israel is the chosen people of God than by the ways of thinking particular to Middle Eastern civilizations, which obviously differ from those of Western cultures. It is this crucial ontological reality—which we are perhaps not accustomed to considering—that places Israel in a unique position before God. Whereas a Gentile people finds it necessary to search for God through philosophical speculation, the chosen people have only to be attentive to the dialogue that is concretized in the covenant, established by God's election and the people's response. Herein is established a particular bond between Israel and God, a bond in which the Lord is particularly close to his people: "I will be your God, and you shall be my people" (Jeremiah 7:23). It is through this bond that Israel becomes and remains "the firstborn" of God.

In other words, a Gentile people's search for God necessarily rests on a speculative plane, while Israel's relationship with God is established through an encounter with a living Person. In the first case, it becomes necessary to prove what one asserts. If God is an assertion of my intellect, then I must demonstrate above all that my assertion is consistent with reality. In the second case, it would be not only irrelevant but also irreverent to try to prove the existence of a God whom I meet in history, a God who enters into living contact with his faithful ones. Such is the case of Israel. It would then be futile to search through prophetic preaching directed to Israel for a speculative demonstration of the existence of God. Likewise, it would be futile to search for it in this book, which seeks to serve the Bible.

The attempt to integrate the Bible with speculative method, trying to prove the existence of God whom we experience as living and life-giving in the pages of the sacred text, would then be the source of the worst sort of confusion. They are two different approaches, both of which are valid and permissible in their own respective arenas, but which cannot be blended together without distorting the Bible and thus robbing it of its fundamentally religious character.

Sofia Cavalletti
Rome
November 1966

Introduction to the Second Italian Edition

When we approach the Bible it is necessary to keep in mind that, in spite of its numerous books, it is nevertheless one book which contains one history and is credited to one principal Author.

As we attempt to say in the following pages, the Bible is understood in light of itself and in its reverberations throughout the life of the believing community, that is, throughout tradition. Hence, we will make references—though undoubtedly insufficient—to the Fathers of the Church and to the liturgy. Such references seek to show how the text has been experienced throughout the centuries, and therefore how it has continued to permeate the life of the believer throughout history. In such an approach, the liturgy is of particular importance, for it is the special place in which the believer encounters the word of God.

Furthermore, it is extremely important to remember that the Bible has always been the book of faith not only for Christians but also for Jews. Due to the limitations of space, we cannot develop this point here but will only make some reference to it, mindful of the fact that this means limiting to some degree the resonance of the biblical text. Were it possible to examine it in the light of the two traditions—Jewish and Christian—the text would assume a greater grandeur before our eyes. Horizons that we have never before pondered would be opened up to us, and thus we would discover with amazement that several passages that are particularly rich in content have held and continue to hold a place of importance in both branches of the people of God.

Furthermore, to complete the picture it would be necessary to keep in mind the importance of the Bible in the Islamic tradition.

Sofia Cavalletti
Rome
July 4, 1986

Chapter 1

The Divine Plan

Open your eyes; the mysteries hidden in the visible are revealed to you.
Gregory of Nyssa

A plan has always existed in the mind of God, the aim of which is to bring humankind to the full enjoyment of God. We usually call this plan "sacred history," or "the history of salvation." The latter term points to the fact that as a result of sin, humankind is in need of salvation in order for the plan of God to be realized in it.

We are familiar with many histories connected to the rise and fall of many peoples, which are limited in time and confined to the boundaries of specific countries. In contrast to these histories, the history of salvation is the history of all peoples and of each person. Its origin stems from the creation of the world. Indeed, there was always present in the mind of God a plan that would unfold in time. Through its realization, people would come to the fullness of life. Differing from the histories of the peoples, which have a beginning, arrive at a point of greatest glory, and then inevitably decline and are replaced by other peoples and civilizations, sacred history follows a progressive development. From creation it is marked by stages that are always ascending toward redemption, in which the divine world and the human world are united in a human being, Jesus of Nazareth.

The Centrality of Redemption

All of creation and all of history reach toward this point of convergence.

Redemption is at the center of history; at the same time it is rooted in the history that precedes it and is also the seed of the history yet to come. Thus, the history of salvation appears to be composed of two phases: the Old Testament and New Testament, which are, in turn, marked by three principal moments: creation, redemption, and Parousia.

We can say that in redemption God's plan reaches its culminating moment in the person of Jesus Christ, and yet awaits the fulfillment of what the gospels call "the Kingdom of God." It is only then that "God will be all in all," and the last enemy, death, will be defeated (I Corinthians 15:24ff.). It is the moment we call the Parousia. We are living in the time of awaiting that moment.

The Principal Moments of the Divine Plan in Its Two Phases

Throughout the history of salvation, divine intervention in human events is constant. Nevertheless, we can pick out certain moments in which this intervention acquires a particular significance. These are particular moments in which God bursts into the history of humankind with a particular force. In these moments it is as if human history is charged with a new surge of power and energy and thus is elevated to a higher plane, empowered to achieve higher objectives.

In this book we will study creation, followed by humankind's initial "no" in the dialogue with God; the universal flood, which marks the reordering of the world following its purification through the destruction of the wicked; the choosing of Abraham and the "yes" of his faith in the ONE God; the revelation of the will of the ONE God through Moses and the solemn vow of Israel to obey God's will; the preaching of the prophets, through whom God educates the hearts of his people toward hope; and the principal events of the life of Christ up to the fulfillment of his mission in the gift of the Holy Spirit as we await the Parousia.

The Two "Branches" of the People of God

The two phases of sacred history differ in a distinctive way. In the first phase God chooses a people: "You shall be for me a priestly kingdom and a holy nation" (Exodus 19:6). God binds the people of Israel to himself in a particular way: "I will be your God, and you shall be my people" (Jeremiah 7:23), entrusting them with a priestly mission.

The phase of salvation history that begins with the coming of Christ is characterized by "the budding of a new branch on the one trunk of the people of God" (John Paul II, May 6, 1982), by the grafting of "a wild olive shoot" (Romans 11:17). At the same time, however, this enrichment has caused the people of God to be torn apart. One branch of God's people—which has drawn a large number of pagans, constituting the church of all nations *(ecclesia ex gentibus)*—has recognized Jesus of Nazareth as the Messiah, the Son of God, while the other branch recognizes Jesus as a prophet, a great teacher in Israel.

Nevertheless, in this situation of schism there does exist a common stretching toward the conclusive moment of history and the full establishment of the reign of God. Both Jews and Christians look toward this moment, even if from different viewpoints. For Christians the Messiah has come, is still coming, and will come again in glory. For Jews the Messiah is yet to come.

This eschatological waiting, though it arises from different motivations, is a gift from God that creates a common expectation in Jews and Christians, as well as a particular way of being and of doing one's daily duties in the history of salvation. The long-awaited Messiah is therefore not only a point of divergence between Jews and Christians, he is also the one who brings them together in waiting for the Parousia, the conclusive moment of history (Document on Ecumenism, Diocese of Rome, 1983).[1]

The Artisans: God and Humankind

From the beginning of the world, up to today, the history of salvation has been gradually constructed through a continuous dialogue between God and humankind. It is a dialogue in which God always has the first word but in which he also awaits the response of all people and of each person. The history of salvation is the history of every person. It requires the contribution of all people for its construction and fulfillment, until the dialogue—in which an ever-increasing number of people throughout the ages will have come to participate—will become a choir singing the praises of God in unison.

Chapter 2

"Sacred History"

History of God, History of Humankind

The peculiar nature of sacred history is implied by its very name, which seems to unite elements derived from two different worlds. When we say "sacred," we mean something pertaining to God. When we say "history," we are referring to the human world, to a series of events bound to time and space, two categories which do not pertain to the world of God. Indeed, the expression "sacred history" could appear to be a contradiction in terms. But it is precisely this apparent contradiction that constitutes the nature of sacred history. We will see that this entanglement of human and divine elements does not represent a contradiction any more than does the concept of the human being, a reality composed of both spirit and body. Just as the person is made up of both spirit and body—if we were to divide the two elements, we would have a cadaver—so sacred history is the indivisible combination of two factors: the work of God and the work of humanity. Therefore, we need two words to define it. It would be a serious error to consider these two elements as separate entities, or to put more emphasis on one than on the other. The work of God and the response of humankind meet and are bound together in the events that make up the history of salvation. This wondrous unity of the human and the divine must not be broken apart lest we distort the true meaning and nature of sacred history.

The Merging of the Temporal and the Eternal

In other words, sacred history is *history* in that it concerns the human world, and it is *sacred* in that God is the principal artisan. Thus, we find in the history of salvation an indivisible union of the human and the divine, the temporal and the eternal, the concrete and the transcendent.

The Temporal and the Eternal in the History of Israel

In the Old Testament, God is revealed first through the work of creation. The mountains, the vast seas, and the stellar distances, become means through which God makes himself known to humankind. In their concrete reality, the rocks and oceans of our world, created in time, become means of revelation and knowledge of God, who is eternal and incomprehensible (Romans 1:19ff.). Then, God links this knowledge of Himself to the history of a people, which shares all the characteristics of the peoples of its time and environment. Israel's history, like that of all peoples, is made up of triumphs and failures. Nevertheless, the fortunes of God and those of Israel are bound together, such that Joshua can turn to the Lord after Israel's defeat and say, "The Canaanites and all the inhabitants of the land will hear of it, and surround us, and cut off our name from the earth. Then what will you to do for your great name?" (Joshua 7:9). In some way, a defeat for Israel also meant a defeat for God, because God wanted Israel's history to be his own history. God desired to be known through the historical events experienced by the chosen people. For instance, in the events of the Exodus, when the will of Pharaoh and will of God for the chosen people clash in a dramatic conflict, we are unable to distinguish between the people's part and God's part. Upon crossing the Red Sea, Israel can sing to the Lord saying, "Your right hand, O Lord, glorious in power—your right hand, O Lord, shattered the enemy" (Exodus 15:6). Yet, the people were not merely passive spectators, but actors fighting with Pharaoh to obtain freedom. They were not only renouncing a life of subjugation; they were also renouncing a life that had provided them certain comforts in a rich country.

In considering the main events of the history of salvation, it is nearly impossible to separate the work of God from that of humankind. It is through this indivisible union that God makes himself known. God who is the Unknowable, Transcendent One makes himself known and ties the knowledge of himself to the tangible and temporal events of human history. In this way the events of history become signs of divine reality. In the study of salvation history, it is necessary to become accustomed to examining historical events for their sake and as signs indicating a reality that transcends them. God is reached through perceivable reality in which he is embodied in a certain way. In other words, God is manifest in a way that we are able to perceive, for we are able to arrive at the transcendent only through the perceivable.

Therefore, we can say that the history of salvation is a "progressive incarnation" of God in human history, by which God makes himself known in the perceivable. Through the events of sacred history, the face of God is being revealed more clearly. Thus, we can say that God is being "incarnated" in history, little by little, in a manner that allows us to perceive him.

If we accept this manner of speaking, if we accept the concept of "progressive incarnation" in history, then we will also understand that the principal event in the history of salvation is the Incarnation in Jesus Christ. "Progressive incarnation" prepared the way and even somehow made it inevitable that God would be manifest so completely, though still through the perceivable and the concrete, namely through the flesh of the Son. There is no longer merely an aspect of God being manifested in the Incarnation, but God's very self.

What is referred to as "the scandal of the Incarnation" is the fact that God, who is transcendent, ties himself to the tangible and the perceivable. God links the manifestation of himself first to creation, then to the history of a people, and finally to a human being. While the manifestation of God in the world may seem most diminished in a human being, it is precisely in the Incarnation of Christ that God's self-manifestation is highest and most perfect.

The Temporal and the Eternal in the Liturgy

Thus, if the Bible demonstrates to us how throughout all of history God has delighted in revealing himself to us through concrete, perceivable elements and events, it should be no surprise that even now God continues to make himself known through the sacraments, in which there is always present a material and perceivable element. The gift of salvation is given to us through water (in Baptism) and is corroborated through bread and wine (in Eucharist).

The Temporal and the Eternal in the Eschatological Period

The same combination of human and divine present throughout history will also be present at the moment of history's consummation. Indeed, Christian hope awaits the resurrection of the body at the time of Parousia, the second coming of Christ. The plan of God is realized not only in the realm of the spirit but in spirit and matter together. As long as the spirit of a person is separated from the body, the salvific plan of God is incomplete and will not be triumphant until God's life-giving power has completely permeated physical matter as well.

If the Incarnation is assigned its true value, then we will recognize an "incarnation"—a manifestation of the transcendent through the perceivable—in the entire life of the people of God, which will continue in the eschatological era.

The Reason: Incarnation

The ultimate reason for the constant presence of a material element in the communication of divine mystery lies in the Incarnation of Christ. This reality is reflected in the life of the church in the consecrated Bread and Wine of the liturgy. Likewise, in the Bible the ultimate reason for the mingling of the human and the divine in history rests always in the Incarnation, which is placed at the center of biblical history. From whatever angle we view this history—from the perspective of the reality we live within the church (the liturgy), or that of the secular preparation for this reality (the Bible)—we always find the focal point to be the figure of Christ, and thus the Incarnation: the eternal and the temporal united in a Person.

Chapter 3

"The Servant of God"

The history of salvation unfolds through the collaboration of God and humankind, but obviously the respective roles are different and unequal. The role of responding to the divine initiative belongs to humankind; the task of being "servants" falls to men and women. This term recurs in the Bible with its own particular meaning, and refers to those individuals who carry particular importance in the history of Israel—those who have a particular mission in its history.

The Meaning of the Expression

In English, when we use the term *servant,* we are primarily expressing a relationship of subordination. The corresponding Hebrew term is connected to the root word from which are derived the verb "to work" and the noun "work." Thus, a more precise translation of the word in English would be "worker" rather than "servant." We could then define "servant" as one who works. But being a servant also means that one does not work on one's own but works *for* and *with* someone. To work *with* someone means that the master and the subordinate work together, with the former directing and supervising and the latter contributing to the job according to his or her own abilities. Furthermore, the product of the servant's work cannot be entirely credited to his or her own merit but reflects the master's role, which the worker must acknowledge. In the encounter between God and human beings in constructing salvation history, God's contribution does not consist merely in initiating the project and inviting others to join in the work. Rather, God also accompanies human beings in the unfolding of their task, while also gradually perfecting their commitment to the initial invitation.

To work *for* a person means that the overall aim of the project does not reside in the one doing the work, but in the intention of the master who proposes it. The aim of sacred history is the salvation of human-kind, so that the love of God might be realized in every human being. The history of salvation is fulfilled in a redeemed humanity, in redeemed persons who have freely given themselves to God and thus have become capable of rendering God praise. The ultimate aim of the history of salvation is the glory of God.

The "Handmaid of the Lord"

In the Bible, Abraham, Moses, the prophets and others are called servants of God. They are all persons who have received an invitation from God to collaborate in a particular way in salvation history. They have accepted their tasks and have committed themselves with their whole lives. The entire people of Israel is God's servant. Among all the peoples of the world, Israel is assigned a priestly mission. The Messiah is also a "servant" of the highest order. Finally, at the threshold of the new order, a special place among God's servants belongs to the Mother of God, who has called herself "the handmaid of the Lord" (Luke 1:38).[2] Whenever the invitation of God is met by a free and full human response, salvation is realized. Except for the response of Jesus, Mary's has been the most perfect response God has ever received from a human creature. Because of her response, Mary was transformed in body and spirit. Because of her "yes," the history of salvation reaches its culminating point.

However, having arrived at its summit the history of salvation does not conclude. It still awaits the collaboration of all people in its diffusion throughout time.If the divine plan unfolds in the Old Testament with the collaboration of humankind, if the Incarnation itself is realized with the participation of human beings, then salvation will continue to be realized in a similar manner in our era, with the free and full response of human beings to God's gift. Each person is offered a work to do in this history, which awaits God's being "all" in every person, and looks forward to God being "all in all."

Chapter 4

Sacred History as Encounter with God

Knowledge That Is Not Speculative, but "Experiential"

Sacred history is God's interaction with human history. In the events of this history, God and humankind are working together, with humankind in the role of "servant" and God as the principal Author who initiates the work and cares for it as it unfolds. Thus, the events of sacred history can be viewed as points of encounter between God and humankind in which humankind comes to know God. For example, the people of Israel live the definitive moment of the Exodus, in which God protects, defends, and helps them. They emerge from this experience with a renewed and deepened knowledge of God, because they have encountered the Lord who, "with strong hand and outstretched arm," has freed them from slavery. They have encountered God working in history.

After such an experience, Israel does not know God merely because it has heard about him; rather, Israel knows God because it encountered him in its own life. Israel's knowledge of God is not merely speculative but is experiential or, more precisely, existential. It is not second-hand knowledge; it is direct knowledge. Israel has not come to an idea about God; rather, Israel has encountered the Person who is alive and at work in history, in Israel's own history. Thereafter, Israel can say with Job, who was instructed by God himself, "I had heard of you by the hearing of the ear, but now my eye sees you" (Job 42:5). God has entered into personal communion with his people.

What has been said about the Exodus can be applied to all the events of sacred history. In these events humankind encounters God and comes to an ever deeper knowledge of him. This knowledge that God bestows on humankind is never abstract, but is tied to and rooted in human life. In the Bible God does not explain who he is in conceptual terms; rather, God enters into communion with human beings, allowing them to experience divine love, justice, and tender mercy.

The words of the prophets clarify the significance of the events. Thus it can be said that God makes himself known through "deeds and words which are intrinsically connected: The works performed by God in the history of salvation show forth and confirm the doctrine and realities signified by the words; the words, for their part, proclaim the works, and bring to light the mystery they contain."[3] The priority given to God's works by the Dogmatic Constitution on Divine Revelation *Dei verbum* is noteworthy (see, for example, 19, ". . . what Jesus . . . really did and taught") and witnesses to a God who is active in the history of humankind, which cannot encounter God except by participating in divine activity. As an active God and a person, God is not known through speculation; rather, God is known by entering into communion with him, assenting to dialogue with him. Friendship with God follows the same rule as friendship with people: One cannot know another person if one has only heard about him or her but has not actually met him or her.

This is of fundamental importance in the reading of the Bible, which should never be merely an academic exercise. In the Bible we will ponder the principal events of the history of salvation. We will study these events in their historical reality, and in them we will meet God. By reflecting on these events, the unfathomable face of God gradually takes shape before us. We do not seek abstract, speculative knowledge from sacred history; rather, we focus on God's work of divine love, justice, and mercy within history. With God's help, the reading of the Bible will then be for us an encounter with the living God.

Chapter 5

The Unity of the Divine Plan

If our reading of the Bible is truly to be an encounter with the living God, we must be aware of the *reality* of the biblical events in our lives. We must realize that those ancient events preserved for us in the Bible are *present* in our lives today in some way. The Bible is largely a historical book, but it is unlike any other book of its kind.

To understand this assertion, it is necessary to keep in mind what was said in the first chapter. The unfolding plan attested to in the Bible is one divine plan, which has its beginning with the creation of the world, passes to a central, definitive moment that we call redemption (in the Incarnation), and will be concluded at the Parousia. Humankind experiences the history of salvation step by step, within the limited confines of its own moment in the history. For the most part, human beings are conscious of what has already been realized, but—with the exception of particular people like the prophets—they are unaware of the future development of sacred history.

Unity of Authorship

Human beings are not the only artisans of sacred history. The other, more important artisan is God, who comprehends in one glance all the millennia being unfolded in history. Throughout this history God intends to realize one aim: the salvation of humankind, the bringing of all people into the fullness of life. In the history of salvation God is like an artist in the process of creating a magnificent work. He alone is responsible for the concept which gives life to the work. Nevertheless, in order to realize the concept, God needs collaborators to whom he entrusts different tasks. These collaborators are human beings who attend to the particular missions assigned to them. They have some knowledge and understanding of what their particular mission is, even though the work in its entirety is beyond their comprehension. In spite of this fact, the masterpiece remains a unified whole.

Unity of Purpose

A single goal, always present in the mind of God, unifies the varied and distant events of history into a whole; namely, that all humankind come to full enjoyment of God. According to Saint Augustine, this goal serves the same function as the golden thread that holds together the pearls of a necklace, without which there would be no unifying object. Without the salvific will of God, history would not be unified.

Salvation history progresses in stages. The preceding stage prepares for the one that follows; each stage contains in itself the stage that preceded it. The Fathers of the Church used the image of the statue, which the artist slowly brings to completion, to explain the stages of salvation history. From a first attempt, the artist moves on to a more refined one; thus, step by step, through succeeding stages that are always more refined, the statue is completed. The first attempt prepares for the finished work, and the finished work contains within itself the first attempt.

The Relationship between the Old and New Testaments

A relationship of this kind binds together the Old and New Testaments and extends into eschatological times. The relationship which binds them is neither one of opposition (as the heretic Marcion of Senopia proposed), nor one of exact identity. Saint Augustine speaks of "consonance," and Saint Irenaeus affirms that "through the polyphony of the words we perceive the unity of one in the same melody."

The time of history in which we are living is the time of expectant waiting. We affirm this during the Eucharistic celebration, when we are invited to proclaim "the Mystery of Faith" and we say: ". . . until You come again." The "statue" will be completed only at the Parousia, the second coming of Christ. We are living in a time when the Sculptor has not yet brought his project to completion.

In the various events that serve as landmarks in the history of salvation, it is important to look for the development of the masterpiece toward perfection. The masterpiece is Christ, the Son of Man, who is the willing, intelligent, perfect instrument of divinity. However, the plan of God is completed not only in a Person, but in the establishment of a Kingdom. In the history of salvation, Christ is like the vital trunk of a plant, out of which comes new life-lines of connection stretching toward that point at which history will be fulfilled. In Christ, salvation history reaches a moment of unique importance, signifying a new, and most particular, instance of divine intervention. But sacred history is not yet completed. The history of salvation continues in every person who enters into the plan of God and participates in it with his or her life.

The Bible and the Liturgy

Believers collaborate in salvation history in a most particular way by living the liturgy, those acts through which the Church makes present Christ's redemptive work in all times and places. Since Christ rooted himself in the history of Israel, the same is true of his "Body," the Church, and of its living actions, which we call liturgy. When we consider the life of the Church, the life we live every day, we search for its roots in the preceding phase of the history of salvation. In the Church's liturgical acts we discover a background covering many centuries, and we find a vastness and grandeur that are perhaps new for us.

The current phase of history also strains toward a fulfillment that will be realized in the Parousia, reaching toward that moment and anticipating it. In the Eucharist the glorified Christ is already present. Eucharist anticipates mysteriously *(sub velo)* the presence of Christ that will be revealed at the Parousia. Therefore, we must keep our focus moving as we consider the life of the Church, considering not only past events but also those of the future, the eschatological realities (from the Greek *eschatos,* meaning "final") that the past events of salvation history have prepared for and anticipated. In this waiting, in this converging toward the eschatological phase—even if from different vantage points—the unity of God's people, Jews and Christians, is being reconstructed.

Therefore, it is important to keep in mind the unity of the divine plan in reading the Bible. By participating in the liturgical life of the Church, we live these events that have come before us, events upon which the Church is founded. At the same time, we look toward the object of all our hope, the Parousia.

At a certain moment in the unfolding of salvation history, each of us made our entrance. Since that moment the Bible has become the book that contains both the prehistory and the history of each of us, and the liturgy is the most particular way in which the events of the Bible are made present once again in our own lives.

Chapter 6

Methodological Principles I: Typology

The way of reading the Bible that we have been describing is that of typology. The term *typology* comes from the Greek *typos* (from the verb *typto,* meaning "to beat"). It refers to the hollow imprint left by a die or mold. The minting of coins is called *typos,* as is the wooden stamp used to make a seal on jars, amphorae, or other vessels.

The typological method is the method of exegesis that either begins with the present phase of salvation history and searches for its roots in the events, institutions, and persons of the Old Testament, or begins with the Old Testament and reads it in light of the events of the New Testament. In other words, the typological method searches for the "imprint" of one phase of sacred history upon another, keeping in mind the unity of the divine plan from creation to Parousia. Just as there is already present in the stamp the image it will leave behind, though it be not fully recognizable, so also the "type" contains the future reality, though in a mysterious way. In the type, the meaningful reality is in seminal form, awaiting development. In some way, the plant to be born is already present in the seed. Though they seem to be two distinct entities, the plant and the seed are intrinsically connected.

Old Testament Typology

The typological method is quite old. The prophets were the first to use it when they spoke of eschatological realities using earlier events as their starting point. For example, in the creation of the heavens and the earth, the prophets saw an initial act that would be completed at the end of time, in a new creation that would renew the heavens and the earth.

New Testament Typology

Typology in the Christian sense of the word is already present in the gospels. Looking forward to the Parousia, typology of this kind sees in Christ and in the Church the fulfillment of the Old Testament. The typological method is also present in the writings and preaching of the Fathers of the Church. In the liturgy the Church is nourished daily by the typological method. Therefore, we can say that the typological method is the Church's method of reading the Bible. Accordingly, it is essential first of all to clarify the significance of typology and describe the span of history being considered. (See chapter seven.)

The Historical Foundation of Typology

The typological method does not detract from the historical reality of the events being interpreted. Indeed, typology cannot be based on anything other than historical facts. Only an event that has truly occurred can be the seed of future events. A plant cannot grow from an imaginary seed. According to Saint Augustine, typology rests "not in words, but in facts" *(non in verbis, sed in facto).*

Liturgy, the Norm of Typology

Naturally, typology has its rules and limitations. Even in referring to the Fathers of the Church, it is necessary to distinguish in their writings between what is their own personal interpretation and what has become the heritage of the Church. The inclusion of some typological interpretations in the liturgy throughout the course of the centuries constitutes a sort of "consecration" of them, so that they can be considered the traditional and official interpretations of the Church. Therefore, the liturgy is the norm in choosing some typological interpretations over others.

The Church has interpreted institutions, events, and persons of the Old Testament according to the typological method. The link which unites the type to the reality being interpreted differs somewhat in each of the three cases.

Typology of Institutions

When dealing with institutions (for example, the sacrifices of Israel), it is necessary first to search for the objective religious meaning that a particular institution had for Israel, and then to seek an analogous institution in Christianity.

Typology of Events

When dealing with events, it is necessary to study the experience of faith that a particular event signifies for Israel. (For example, what did the Exodus from Egypt represent in the religious life of the Hebrew people?) Only then can they be compared to analogous events in Christian religious experience—both to current realities and to those of the end times.

Typology of Persons

Finally, it is necessary to study the religious significance a specific person's work has for Israel's history, in order to see whether it corresponds in part to the mission carried out by Jesus and continued in the Church. It will then be possible to establish the content and the limits of such correspondence.

Chapter 7

The Three Stages of Typology

Christian typology has all too often been limited to a typology of two stages—that is, one that considers only the current moment of history without taking into account the unity of the entire divine plan from creation to Parousia. Yet, the correct use of such an interpretive method leads one to a typology of *three* stages, one that embraces the eschatological reality we await, properly balancing the history that has already been realized and the one that lies before us.

Dei verbum (3,13) points to "the unity of all of Scripture" as "the interpretative means of reading it."

Typology in the Church

Although we have too often limited ourselves to a typology of two stages, there are plenty of examples of three-stage typology in the tradition of the Church. For instance, Origen writes:

> Why must the paschal meal be eaten at sunset? Because the Lord suffered the passion at the sunset of the world, in order that you might always be able to eat the flesh of the Word, and because you are always in the evening until the morning comes. . . . You will rejoice in the morning which is the second coming.[4]

He goes on to say,

> If you could penetrate the heavens with your mind and spirit and follow Jesus Christ who has penetrated the heavens . . . you would find there those riches of which the Law was but a shadow and the image of which Christ revealed in the Incarnation, those riches which God has prepared for the blessed ones.[5]

Even more explicitly, Saint Ambrose speaks of "the shadow of the Law, the image in the Gospel, the truth in the heavenly realities."[6] There is also the prayer that follows the reading of Exodus 14:15—15:1 at the Easter Vigil in which the three stages of history are specifically mentioned:

> O God, whose ancient wonders
> remain undimmed in splendor even in our day,
> for what you once bestowed on a single people,
> freeing them from Pharaoh's persecution
> by the power of your right hand,
> now you bring about as the salvation of the nations
> through the waters of rebirth,
> grant, we pray, that the whole world
> may become children of Abraham
> and inherit the dignity of Israel's birthright.

Typology in the Synagogue

A similar typological interpretation involving projection to the end times, one that is consistent with a true Christian typology, is preserved in the reading of the Bible in the synagogue. This interpretation echoes the way the prophets interpreted ancient events.

In the synagogue rite celebrated in Italy, for example, after the account of the flood (Genesis 6:9—11:32), the prophetic reading *(haftarah)* from Isaiah 54:1—55:5 is read. From a world renewed by the waters of the flood, but which has then fallen back into disorder at the Tower of Babel, there opens a vision of the new Jerusalem, which will be rebuilt with precious stones, sapphires, and rubies. This vision includes the promise of an everlasting "covenant of peace."

In the same rite, after the account of Joseph (Genesis 44:18—47:27), which concludes with the coming of the Israelites to Egypt, the prophetic reading from Ezekiel 37:15—38:12 is read. This passage announces the return of the children of Israel to their land from the countries where they had been dispersed. When they return, "[God's] servant David" will be their shepherd.

The Jewish and Christian peoples, these two peoples of the Book, read the Bible with a similar methodology. Both peoples are searching for the "golden thread" that binds together the history that God is creating with humankind.

The Church and the Synagogue thus converge in their way of approaching the word of God and in their projection toward the eschatological phase of history. In the synagogue the Bible is read in two stages, going directly from the events of Israel's history to the end times. The Church, which sees in Christ and the realities connected to him a pivotal moment of history, adopts a typology of three stages.

As noted above, it is necessary to identify the span of history being considered in typological interpretation. A typology that does not go beyond the present Christian realities is a typology divested of hope and impairs the very plan of God.

Only by considering sacred history in its entirety is it possible to penetrate, however slowly, the meaning of the events comprising that history and, in some way, to understand the plan of God, in which all people are invited to collaborate.

Only a typological reading of the Bible will enable us to draw near to the mystery of God, because God makes himself known to us through his works. Only this type of interpretation teaches us, in the words of Hans Urs von Balthasar, "to know the heart of God, to share in God's thoughts about the world."

The charge of mystery, which fills the pages of the Bible, will be revealed to us only if we are able to view the events of sacred history against the cosmic backdrop of the entire plan of God.

Chapter 8

Typology and Memorial

In the celebration of the memorial of Jesus' Passover, the Last Supper, the liturgy has accustomed us to living the events of the past in the present, while turning us toward eschatological times. In order to realize this, it is necessary to be somewhat familiar with the Jewish Passover celebration and with the Eucharist. In some way, the celebration of the memorial annihilates time in some way, making present today the events of the past, events which without the celebration would be lost forever. The memorial also projects these events toward the end times and, in so doing, prepares for the completion of history.

Thus, to speak of the memorial, one must use the same terms as those used in relation to typology. Both memorial and typology exhibit a kind of freedom from time; the distance between events seems to disappear, and the events merge into one unified expression of God's salvation and love, in which past and future are fused. Both typology and memorial exercise this freedom. Indeed, it seems that only in such a state of freedom can they be what they truly are. Memorial concretizes in the present the salvation already expressed in preceding events and thus also prepares for the moment of eschatological completion, anticipating it and preparing for it in prayer and hope. In the same way, as it interprets the Bible read in the present, typology ties together the preceding history with the object of our hope, that "golden thread,"[7] as Saint Augustine calls it: the aim of God that makes one history out of so many diverse events.

Accordingly, it is important to consider the bond that unites typology and memorial. They have the same characteristics and so must be linked to one another at a very deep level. But what links them? And at what deep level?

The Constitution on the Sacred Liturgy (Sacrosanctum concilium (48–51)), speaks of the "table" of the word and the "table" of the body of the Lord. There is therefore one "table" around which we draw near to the mystery of God: the Word and the Sacrament. Thus, it seems to be in the oneness of that "table" that typology and memorial find their unity and their likeness to one another. Such a likeness is born from within them, springing from the one source of revelation that they share.

The Mystery Heard and Celebrated

Typology and memorial are bound together at the level of the Reality that draws us near: the infinite mystery of God. The mystery speaks and acts. One reaches it by listening and participating in the sacramental celebration. When the mystery speaks and we listen to it, the method of listening is that of typology. When the mystery is celebrated and we participate in it, the way of participating is memorial. Whether we are listening to the word or participating in the sacramental celebration, the reality we are living is the same: the one table of the Word and of the Body of the Lord. If the table is one, then the rules of the table must be the same. In order to comprehend and live God's message, we need one methodology that helps us penetrate its "globality" as we experience sacred history, with both its past and future dimensions brought together in the present moment.

In this regard, typology appears to be no less essential than memorial in drawing us into the mystery. Typology is not an arbitrary method of reading, nor a scholarly gimmick. Rather, it is that way of reading scripture that is demanded by the Bible's very contents: the way that is essentially appropriate to the Word of God. No faithful reading can exclude typology. A reading of the Bible that truly aims at scrutinizing and penetrating the Mystery cannot be done without typology, just as the sacramental celebration of that same mystery cannot be done other than in the memorial.

It is not without reason that the typological method is found in the two traditions that are based on the Bible: Judaism and Christianity. However, just as the memorial enables us to live the celebrated event in the present, making present the past and opening the doors of eschatological hope, so also, from the Christian perspective, typological interpretation must be done *in three stages* if it is to be a help to us in drawing into that Word through which God is manifest.

Regrettably, typology has not always been applied in this way, and the resulting theological and practical consequences have been quite serious: a weakening of hope, a loss of dynamism in the expectation of the "new heavens and the new earth," and, in relation to Israel, the emergence of a "theology of substitution." This "theology of substitution" has said: At *one time* there was Israel, *now* there is the Church. And this theology has brought about what has been referred to as "the teaching of contempt," which was the attempt to remove Israel from the divine plan. The theological and practical consequences of this way of thinking have been extremely grave.

Chapter 9

Creation

ESSENTIAL TEXT TO BE READ: Genesis 1:1—2:25

The history of salvation begins with the creative act of God. The Bible has preserved for us two accounts of creation which differ in origin and nature. The first account is recorded in Genesis 1:1—2:3, and the second in Genesis 2:4–25. Since the creation accounts are found in the first pages of the Bible, and since they deal with primordial events, one might easily assume that they are the oldest biblical texts; yet this is not the case. On the contrary, these texts represent a point of arrival in biblical theology.[8]

The Literary Genre

What is contained in the first and second chapters of Genesis is obviously not a chronicle of the events of creation as recorded by eyewitnesses. Rather, in these chapters we find the response Israel has given to the basic questions, "Where did the world come from? Where did human-kind come from?" But Israel has answered these questions as only the chosen people—a people who find themselves in a special relationship with God—could answer. Even the formulation of the question springs from this relationship. Israel has not asked the question out of mere intellectual curiosity, but as a result of having been placed in a particular listening stance before God.

Therefore, the creation accounts in Genesis are the product of God's work within a human author, a process called *inspiration*. This means that the text has been written with particular guidance from God, such that God is in some way its author. For this reason, it constitutes for the believer a solid teaching, as the Church has taught through the centuries.

The God we meet in these pages of Genesis is "the God of our fathers," the "God of Abraham, of Isaac, and of Jacob," the God with whom Israel has already had a long experience. The creation accounts assert that the God whom Israel met as its liberator in its first religious experience is also creator of the universe. While this creator is the same God Israel has known in its history, the creation accounts reflect Israel's new understanding of its God.

The power that the Lord demonstrated in freeing Israel from slavery in Egypt is revealed in Genesis in the work of creation. That goodness, that providential care God showed toward Israel, is here focused on Adam—on humankind itself—for whom all of creation has been called into being. Finally, here God is presented above all as ONE in overwhelming power and providential goodness. Indeed, the creation accounts echo the preaching of the prophets. In creation the horizon of sacred history is expanded beyond the restricted arena of Israel's history to include all people. The creation accounts attest to the full maturity of the Hebrew people's monotheism, so that it can be said: There is no Lord besides the one God.

The texts in question bear the characteristics of the literary genre of wisdom literature, because they are the fruit of meditation. But they are wisdom texts that are strongly influenced by the prophets.

Examination of the Texts: The First Account

The first account of creation has the grandeur of a text carved in stone.

The refrain "and there was evening and there was morning" rhythmically punctuates the intervals between God's creative acts. The prompt obedience of things to the creative word ("And it was so") is the incisive expression of the power of God, whose commands do not allow for delays. The phrase "God saw that it was good" after each creative act underscores the positive nature of creation. In God, goodness accompanies power; thus, the wondrous work of creation is done for humankind and is placed at their disposal.

"In the beginning" indicates the beginning of the creative activity of God, who obviously precedes the creative activity. Recent biblical studies have shown that the phrase commonly translated "the earth was a formless void" is more accurately rendered "the earth was nothingness." In other words, there is no allusion to chaos in the text, but rather to the fact that God created the earth from nothing. In fact, the Hebrew word for the verb *create* is used in the Bible only in reference to the creative act of God, thus distinguishing it from human activity.

"Day" and "week" are basic divisions of time and are not to be taken literally. The statement in Genesis 2:2 that God "rested on the seventh day" suggests the projection of Israel's religious practices into the text. For the author of this story, the observance of the sabbath is not meant to be taken merely as a duty in the covenant with God, but as a cosmic reality reflected in the life of the people.

When God creates animals on the earth (Genesis 1:22), God blesses them with solemn words that are similar to the blessing given to humankind (1:28). The appearance of the first living creatures is a great event. In a previously immobile world, creatures now move about, responding as they are able to the voice of God.

The Creation of Humankind

Only in the creation of humankind, however, does God say, "Be masters of the fish of the sea, the birds of heaven, and all living animals on the earth." In fact, the first account of creation tends to underscore the special position of humankind among the creatures. Human beings are created last because everything is ordered for them. The progressive unfolding of the work of creation is aimed at the preparation of an environment suitable to humankind.

The unique position of humankind is further underscored by the words, "Let us make humankind in our image . . ." (1:26). With these words God decisively sets humankind apart from the rest of creation because humankind carries within itself the image of God; humankind bears the likeness of God ("image and likeness" are analogous terms used to reinforce the meaning). Thus, God places humanity "on the same side" as God, set apart from the rest of creation. The sacred author repeats the assertion in verse 27 to make it clear that if an image of God exists in the world, it exists in humankind.

This elevation of humankind over the animals perhaps echoes the prohibition in the Mosaic Law against using animal images as images of the divine in worship.

Examination of the Texts: The Second Account

The second account of creation (Genesis 2:4–25) differs a great deal from the first. In the first account humankind appears as the completion of the work of creation, like the final and distinctive note of a grand symphony. In the second account the creation of the subhuman world is only briefly mentioned in order to concentrate on the condition of humankind before sin. Therefore, the second account also serves as a prelude to the account of sin.

A certain imbalance among the elements of the second account, as well as the presence of several repetitions, indicates that it is a composite text. A comparison of this text with extra-biblical texts demonstrates that the author has drawn from the traditional narrative heritage of the ancient Middle East, adapting that heritage to his own purposes, and yet also including entire passages without modification (such as the description of the rivers of the Garden of Eden in Genesis 2:11–14). Moreover, a basic knowledge of the creation myths of the ancient Middle East is sufficient for identifying the sources of the biblical text. For instance, we read in Genesis 2:4–5,

> In the day that the Lord God made the earth and the heavens, when no plant of the field was yet in the earth and no herb of the field had yet sprung up— for the Lord God had not caused it to rain upon the earth, and was there no one to till the ground. . . .

Here we encounter the well-known Babylonian creation myth that begins with the words, "When the heavens had not yet been named"— that is, when they did not exist—"when not even the earth had been named. . . ." The biblical inability to represent nothingness, expressed as a negation of existence, also exists in the Babylonian text.

The Doctrine

The doctrine of this second account of creation can be found in the way the author speaks of humankind *(adam),* placing human beings in relation to the earth *(adamah):* "The Lord God formed man *(adam)* from the dust of the ground *(adamah)*" (Genesis 2:7). Humankind is essentially of the earth, made from the soil, and placed by God in the Garden of Eden on a superior plane to the rest of nature. But humankind sins, and so God says to them, "You are dust, and to dust you shall return" (Genesis 3:19).

What the author seeks to relate in the second account is a parable about human beings in general, lifted up by God and yet incapable of keeping themselves in the position in which divine goodness placed them. The description of the garden of delights emphasizes what God had offered; it also makes the fall more dramatic.

The Creation of Woman

Alongside this central theme is placed the creation of woman, which is presented in the first account simultaneously with the creation of man ("male and female he created them," Genesis 1:27). The second account concludes that man and woman are intimately connected by their very nature; they are "one flesh," such that the man can say of the woman, "This at last is bone of my bones and flesh of my flesh; this one shall be called woman *(ishah),* for out of man *(ish)* this one was taken" (Genesis 2:23). Thus, the close relationship that unites man and woman is also expressed by the words used to identify them. In view of such a relationship, it is then only natural that men and women are attracted to each other, leaving their original families to form new unions.

The author describes the creation of woman as occurring while the man was sleeping, perhaps establishing a correlation between the creation of woman and the birth of a child. Just as a child is born from the darkness of the maternal womb, so also the woman is created during the "deep sleep" of Adam. Just as the child is born from the organs of the mother, so Eve is formed from the "rib" of the man. Finally, just as the child is part of the mother and yet is distinct from her, so also the woman is part of the man but is distinct from him.

The "deep sleep" of Adam is expressed with a word that also has a religious significance in Hebrew. It indicates a certain receptive passivity on the part of the human being, which makes it possible for God to work in him or her.

Chapter 10

The Typology of Creation

After considering, however briefly, the account of creation in itself, both in terms of its fundamentally Jewish doctrine and of its background in Middle Eastern culture, we must consider the creation account in relation to the history of salvation, asking if and how creation is reflected in the cosmic development of sacred history toward its eschatological completion.

Therefore, the second stage of interpretation will consist of asking whether the figure of Jesus in some way corresponds to a figure in creation (Christological typology), and whether something in the creation account is the seed of the sacraments that we live in the Church today (sacramental typology).

These two quests are two aspects of one reality: Christ, who is inseparable from his Body, the Church, which lives its relationship with God in a particular way through those acts Christ does for and with humanity: the sacraments. This reality is rooted in the Old Testament and is projected toward the eschatological phase of history.

Christological Typology: Jesus and Adam

The figure of Adam dominates the account of creation and presents a typology that has two aspects. The first aspect is one of correspondence to Jesus: Adam is the first human and thus the firstborn of creation; Jesus is the firstborn of the world that has entered a new phase of creation with redemption. The second aspect is one of contrast: Adam is the sinner, and Jesus is the one who restores what was damaged by Adam's sin.

For now we will stop at the first point and consider 1 Corinthians 15:45ff. Here, Saint Paul speaks of Adam as a man "from the earth," signifying not only where he came from but also the material used in his creation (*adamah,* Hebrew for "earth"). Adam is "the man of dust" (verse 48), as are his descendants, who are "of the dust." Christ, however, is "of heaven," both in his origin and his substance. He is "the man of heaven," and so also those who are united with him by faith will become "heavenly." With Christ's resurrection the second creation is initiated. The new creation is a re-creation of the first, but on a higher plane. Those who have carried in themselves the image of the "earthly man" will now bear the image of the one who is "from heaven" (verse 49).

This same typology is present in the liturgy. The prayer that accompanies the preparation of the chalice in the Missal of Pius V reads, "Lord God, the creation of man was a wonderful work, his redemption still more wonderful."

Sacramental Typology: Baptism and the Life-giving Waters of Creation

The sacramental typology of creation is essentially related to baptism. The gift of eternal life is given to us through the waters of baptism. "No one can enter the kingdom of God without being born of water and Spirit" (John 3:5).

In order that we might be prepared to live this wonder, water has had a lifegiving power since the earliest times.

> O Man, you must venerate the age of water, the antiquity of this substance. Venerate also its benefits, because it has been the seat of the divine spirit who thus preferred it to the other elements. The darkness was without form, without the adornment of the stars, the abyss was deep, the earth not formed, the heavens were shapeless; only water, the perfect material since the beginning, fertile and simple, was stretched out over all, transparent, like a throne worthy of God. . . .

As soon as the world was ordered in its various elements so that it could be given inhabitants, the waters were the first element to receive the order to produce living creatures. It is this first water that gave birth to whatsoever is living; so then, there is no need to be astonished if the baptismal waters still generate life.[9]

In speaking of the creation of animals, Saint Ambrose says, "They were born at the beginning of creation, but for you were reserved the waters that regenerate you through grace, just as they generated life for the animals." As the fish swims in the water and also in the storms, he writes, so may "you too be a fish so that the waves of the world do not engulf you."[10]

It is particularly significant that the account of creation (Genesis 1:1—2:3) is read at the Easter Vigil, the night in which the baptismal waters are consecrated and the catechumens are baptized. Why does the liturgy take us back to the creation of the world when we have gathered to celebrate the Resurrection of Christ? The answer lies in the prayer mentioned above: "Lord God, the creation of man was a wonderful work, his redemption still more wonderful." In other words, redemption is a new creation.

Later in the Easter Vigil, in the prayer of consecration of the baptismal water, we find the words: "O God, whose Spirit in the first moments of the world's creation hovered over the waters, so that the very substance of water would even then take to itself the power to sanctify. . . ." The liturgy considers the initial moments of salvation history alongside the moment of redemption in one unified history in which the different events are bound together by the plan of God that is being unfolded.

Chapter 11

Creation and Parousia

Although redemption is a determinant point, it is not the final one. For this reason it is necessary to consider the New Testament not only by looking at what has preceded it, but also by turning toward the future. Christianity is not a point of arrival at which we come to a halt; rather, it is a point of departure. It is dynamic and momentous; it is a hope for the completion of what has already occurred, a waiting for the complete realization of all that has been accomplished in Jesus. Only with this cosmic vision will history acquire its full dynamism, the hope of humankind be nourished, and the work of humankind find its true value.

Jesus is already the perfect *human being* who announces and anticipates in himself in a perfected *humanity*. Therefore, Christianity is essentially the anticipation of the moment in which "God will be all in all."

The prophets speak of this final point, the Parousia. But who are the prophets, and how do they know about the Parousia? "Prophet" means "one who speaks for another"—in this case, for God. For now, we will limit ourselves to addressing what they say for God regarding the Parousia.

Eschatology and the First Events

How can the prophets know about future events? The scriptures report that God gives them knowledge of these things: "The Lord of hosts has sworn in my hearing . . ." says Isaiah (5:9). Thus, the prophet could rely on the authority of God and ask us to accept blindly what he says, renouncing our desire to understand. Yet, the prophet does not ask his hearers to sacrifice the intellect. Instead, the prophet asks for an open mind that will allow us to penetrate the true nature of things. One might also say that the prophet asks of us a power of vision that enables us to see beyond the veil of the future, and thus to know and penetrate the secrets of the divine will.

Hence, the prophets tell us about the things of the future—things that are unknown—and offer us proof of these things. What proof? Basing their claims upon events which have already occurred and can be verified, the prophets tell us that these known historical facts allow us to know God (therein revealing God's power, goodness, and so forth). Therefore, they ask, is it not possible that God, who has already been powerful, good, and so forth, could be so again, and to an even greater degree? Could those marvelous acts of God, such as creation, not be repeated on an even higher level? Has God's power been exhausted in what he has already done? "Is my hand shortened, that it cannot redeem? Is the Lord's power limited?" (Isaiah 50:2; Numbers 11:23).

From past events the prophets infer that the divine power manifested in history will produce even greater results in the future. God's marvelous deeds, the *mirabilia Dei,* are not ends in themselves but constitute a seed that must germinate and develop. In looking at the seed, we are able to imagine what the fruit will be like.

The prophets thus speak to us of the first events in order to speak to us of the final ones. They are faithful to the basic principle of biblical method, that of being concrete. They never depart from it, even when it seems most difficult to remain anchored in the concrete. How does one remain concrete when speaking of things of the future? When speaking of future—therefore unknown—things, the things that are known must serve as the springboard. The unknown things of the future are deduced from the known things of the past.

The Renewal of Creation

The texts available regarding the renewal of creation are numerous. We will limit ourselves to some of the more important ones.

The Lord created the world in which we live. This is a given. Therefore, it should not be surprising when God says through the mouth of the prophet: "For I am about to create new heavens and a new earth; the former things shall not be remembered or come to mind" (Isaiah 65:17). The renewed creation will be so great that the first one will be erased from human memory. Some of the most evident aspects of renewed creation will be harmony between people and animals, as in the Garden of Eden before humans sinned (Isaiah 11:6ff.), the great bounty of the fruits of the earth (Amos 9:13ff.) due to the extraordinary abundance of water (Ezekiel 47:12; Isaiah 41:18ff.; Zechariah 14:8), and the transformation of nature (Isaiah 60:19, 20).

The Abundance of the Spirit of God

The Spirit of God appears in the work of creation at the beginning, bringing life to the natural world. The principal life-giving agent of the new creation will also be the Spirit: "When you send forth your spirit [or breath], they are created; and you renew the face of the ground" (Psalm 104:30). However, the new creation will be distinguished by a particular abundance of the Spirit, such that what was previously reserved for a privileged few will now be a gift that reaches out to all.

> Then afterward I will pour out my spirit on all flesh; your sons and your daughters shall prophesy, your old men shall dream dreams, and your young men shall see visions. Even on the male and female slaves I will pour out my spirit." (Joel 2:28–29)

Saint Peter cites this prophetic passage of Joel in his first sermon to the crowds at Pentecost (see Acts 2:14ff.). He proclaims that what the prophet announced is now being realized, because the messianic times have begun.

The Spirit that begins to rest on all people on Pentecost is the same Spirit that had come to rest on the Messiah, the firstborn of the new creation (Matthew 3:16). In the desert "he was with the wild beasts" (Mark 1:13). At another moment, the disciples, still not grasping who Jesus really was, asked, "What sort of man is this, that even the winds and the sea obey him?" (Matthew 8:27). He is the fountain from which "will flow rivers of living water"; thus, he is the one who can say to the crowd: "Let anyone who is thirsty come to me!" (John 7:37).

All this happened because the Spirit of God rested on him from the moment of his conception, enriching him in a particular way at his baptism in the Jordan, and fully mastering and transforming his humanity at the moment of the resurrection. Therefore, those elements that humankind awaits at the end of time are realized in the person of Jesus. Until now, the plan of God has been fully realized only in him. Christian hope is directed toward the time when God's plan will have reached all of creation—all people and all things (Romans 8:19).

Chapter 12

Methodological Principles II: The Literary Genre

The Author's Intention and the Literary Genre

Before considering the other principal moments in the history of salvation, it is important to deal with a question of methodology, specifically that of the literary genre.

Already on the first pages of Genesis there are problems of interpretation that could be synthesized into one question: What did the author intend to say? The question will become even more persistent in relation to the pages dedicated to original sin, which speak of the "forbidden fruit," the "tree of the knowledge of good and evil," the "serpent," and so forth.

In order to respond to the question of the author's intention, one must first deal with the question of the literary genre of the text. For example, a poet can use images that would not be suitable in prose writing. Likewise, the form used in a historical account will differ from that used in a simple narration or an editorial. The Bible is a vast collection of writings that are diverse in origin and character, and thus cannot all be evaluated in the same way.

Every time we open the Bible, we must ask the questions. What was the intention of the author? Did the author intend to write a chronicle, to give a teaching, to analyze something?

In addition, it is also important to consider the culture which produced the text in question. The form that a literary genre takes in one cultural setting can differ from the form it takes in another. Sometimes the very criteria used to determine the genre differs. For example, the modern historical genre differs profoundly from the style of ancient historical accounts. After ascertaining the literary genre of a particular text, one must seek to discover the form it takes in its particular cultural setting.

A Common Literary Form

Israel is a people of a particular time and cultural setting whose language and mode of expression are similar to those of its neighbors. The Semitic languages share great similarity in structure and vocabulary. The languages themselves are alike, as well as the particular expressions that reveal the people's way of thinking. Therefore, in order to fully understand the message Israel has transmitted, we must leave the confines of biblical literature and study the forms of expression that were common in the ancient Middle East.

The Constitution on Divine Revelation (Dei verbum, 12) says that, in the Bible, God has spoken "through human beings in human fashion." This recalls what Pius XII taught in the famous encyclical Divino Afflante Spiritu:

> The interpreter [of scripture] must, as it were, go back wholly in spirit to those remote centuries of the East and, with the aid of history, archaeology, ethnology and other sciences, accurately determine what modes of writing, so to speak, the authors of that ancient period would be likely to use, and in fact did use. For the ancient peoples of the East, in order to express their ideas, did not always employ those forms or manner of speaking which we use today but those used by the people of their times and countries. What those were exactly the commentator can only determine after a careful examination of the ancient literature of the East. The investigation on this point, which has been carried out during the past forty or fifty years with greater care and diligence than ever before, has more clearly shown what forms of expression were used in those far off times, whether in poetic description, or in the formulation of laws and rules of life, or in recording the facts and events of history (35–36).

Singular in Concept

Singular in concept and written in the common language: here we find another aspect of the human and divine character presented to us in the

Bible. Mind of God, Word of God, revelation of God, the Bible reaches humankind through human language. Although the revelatory word of God is unique and cannot be compared to any other literature, the finite human word is expressed in a form and structure that any Semitic person of the period might have used. Thus, in order to reach the word of God, one must know and experience the word of humans.

Word of God and Human Word

The biblical texts are similar in literary form to the pagan texts of the ancient Middle East, though they differ profoundly in content. Israel expresses concepts (such as monotheism, which is the fundamental reality and the particular concept that is the core of the Bible's uniqueness) in the common language of its time and setting. Yet, the concepts themselves are *not* of Israel's time and setting. One reaches biblical thought, which is unique, through language that is common to the peoples of the ancient Semitic East. Thus, in order to understand the Bible, one must know the setting in which Israel lived and how the peoples close to Israel lived and spoke.

Once again, it is in the person of Christ, in the Incarnation, that we find clarification on the precise nature of the Bible as the Word of God and the human word. As the encyclical of Pius XII affirms, Jesus was human like us in all ways except our sinfulness. Furthermore, the Bible speaks the language of human beings, but without error. In order for the word of God to be expressed understandably to human beings, it required a "body." This body was found in the Semitic setting, and in this setting the word is "incarnated," conserving the uniqueness of the thought being expressed. The Bible, Word of God and human word, transcends and surpasses time and space. Yet at the same time it clearly bears the imprint of the historical time and cultural setting in which it was written.

Therefore, for us to understand a biblical text, it is not enough to isolate the literary genre and to know the form it took in the ancient Middle East, although this work is preliminary and indispensable. Such work alone will not reveal the spirit of the biblical text. In order to perceive the spirit of the text, "one must be very diligent in paying attention to the contents of the text and the unity of all Scripture" (*Dei verbum,* 12).

Given the uniqueness of the biblical message, nothing can better aid the understanding of it than the Bible itself. References to an extra-biblical text will not lead us to fuller doctrinal comprehension of the Bible. Such references are only indirectly useful in lending greater emphasis to the truth of God's word and to its eternal reality. Thus, in comparison with the Bible, the thinking behind such extra-biblical texts—with their merely partial truths—has long since been surpassed. Revelation cannot be illuminated except by revelation itself. We must not be fearful of approaching texts of varying characters and dates, keeping in mind that the Bible is one unique book and that it is always the same Spirit who speaks in it. For knowledge of the external form of the texts, we must go outside the Jewish world and enter the world we call "the biblical setting," the civilization in which the Jewish people lived. However, to discover the doctrine in the texts, we must not go beyond the confines of the Bible, because the word of God contained therein is unique and cannot be compared to anything else. Although we are searching for the message of salvation that God has revealed to humankind in the biblical literature, both investigations are necessary because an ignorance of the exterior form the message has assumed would compromise the accurate understanding of the doctrine.

It has been said that "it is impossible to understand God without first understanding Israel" (Renckens)[11] and the setting in which Israel lived, because the divine message has assumed a clearly individualized form, and this form is characteristically Jewish.

Chapter 13

The Account of Original Sin

ESSENTIAL TEXT TO BE READ: **Genesis 3**

The account of original sin not only follows the second account of creation but is an integral part of it. The accounts of creation offer the first realization of God's plan. They present human beings as having the dignity of privileged creatures who have every element of creation placed at their disposal and who live in a marvelous world created for them by God.

However, the collaboration of humankind is required in order for God's plan to be realized. In sinning, created human beings deny their "servanthood" in the fulfillment of God's plan. In reading the scriptural text, the methodological principles set forth in the preceding chapter are immediately applicable. The texts under consideration are identified as wisdom literature with strong prophetic influences. The author wants to explain the reasons for the state of humankind and the world. To discern the validity of the teaching presented in the text, we return to what was said in reference to the account of creation: There are expressions and images in the text that are difficult to interpret, even though the images themselves are familiar to us. Thus, we will first consider the literature of the ancient Middle East to see if it can offer help in interpreting the biblical account of sin.

A Babylonian Epic

An ancient Babylonian epic focuses on a hero named Gilgamesh. In it, the hero becomes troubled upon the death of a friend. It seems to be

Gilgamesh's first experience of death, and he suddenly finds himself before a reality that frightens him with its inescapable harshness.

The apparition of his friend's spirit arouses within Gilgamesh a desire for eternal life. He seeks the advice of a sage who appears to have attained it. The sage tells Gilgamesh to search for a plant similar to the hawthorn tree whose needle "pierces the hand like a rose," a plant that will give him eternal life. After finding the plant, Gilgamesh returns home. In the course of his journey, he becomes thirsty and goes down to bathe in the waters of a roadside well. At that moment a *serpent* is attracted by the fragrance of the plant and seizes it. The defeated hero is undone over the loss of the plant and its gift of eternal life, now gone forever.

Formal Elements in the Biblical Account

We cannot fail to notice several connections between this text and the biblical account, even if they are only literary in nature. The Babylonian epic speaks of a "plant of life," an image that attempts to give form to an elusive principle. The hero desires life itself, which the author expresses in the symbol of a plant. This symbol is similar to that of the "fountain of life," which also seeks to embody an elusive concept. The Bible's "tree of life" and "tree of the knowledge of good and evil" do not refer to actual plants. These images seek to render something that is intangible evident and concrete. Their intended meaning is that of a "spring" or source of life and unlimited knowledge. In fact, the two opposites, good and evil, are intended to indicate totality.[12]

An important character in the story is the serpent. In the Semitic world, the serpent is a demonic being that often plays an important part in the practice of magic. Thus, guile was a characteristic often given to the serpent in ancient literature, as in the biblical account when it deceives the woman into breaking God's command ("You will not die but you will become like God"). The literary use of the serpent can be seen as a challenge to those peoples who believed the serpent to be a god of the underworld. The human couple's shame after sinning because of their nakedness can be interpreted in light of other biblical texts in which slaves were nude as they worked (Deuteronomy 28:48). Nudity in this case is a sign of slavery and humiliation.

The Doctrine: God and Humankind

Having considered the formal elements of the story, in which knowledge of the Bible's cultural setting has been helpful, it is now possible to reflect on the doctrine contained in the biblical account. It is useless to search through parallel pagan texts for this purpose. Babylonian literature contains nothing that can be compared to the doctrinal content of biblical text. When the Babylonian account of creation arrives at the creation of human beings, sin already reigns in the world, introduced by the gods themselves. The presence of evil in the world is not attributed to humans in the Babylonian myth; rather, it is the sole responsibility of the gods.

In the Bible, however, humankind takes responsibility for the evil that reigns in the world. God is in no way responsible for it. The scripture scholar Tresmontant has suggested that humanity reaches an adult consciousness in this account, maturely accepting personal responsibility without trying to blame others. If there is evil in the world, God has no part in it. Humankind has brought evil into creation through a conscious and deliberate act. The God of the prophets' preaching and the psalmists' prayer is here, the God who does not tolerate iniquity and before whom not even the highest heavens are pure. Before this God humankind can only say: "Both we and our ancestors have sinned" (Psalm 106:6).

Sin

The prohibition against eating the fruit of the tree of the knowledge of good and evil indicates that limits are placed on humankind by their very nature as creatures. Unlimited knowledge can belong only to God. As we have seen, humankind's role in the divine plan is that of "servant," with all the dignity and the limitations that such a role implies. In defying God's prohibition, humankind refuses to accept its true condition as creature. According to the doctrine Israel is expressing here, sin is a personal, voluntary act through which humankind enters into conflict with God. This is far from the understanding of sin widespread in the ancient Middle East, according to which sin is something external to humankind, an evil that can rise up in human beings without their even knowing how. Such a belief is not corroborated in even the oldest parts of the Bible.

The Consequences of Sin

The first consequences of sin involve the curse of the earth. A mysterious solidarity exists between the earth and humankind. The perfect state in which humankind existed in the Garden of Eden ("every kind of tree, enticing to look at and good to eat") was contingent on humankind's innocence. Nature was placed at the disposal of innocent humankind because nature was created for the sake of human beings.

For the Earth

The internal disorder of humankind is projected onto the earth, resulting in disorder in nature. Hence, the earth will yield only "brambles and thistles" for humans. The harmony that was meant to have bonded humanity and the earth in common service to God is shattered. Instead, a state of rebellion rises up in nature, which human beings contaminated through their disobedience (Romans 8:20).

For the Serpent

The serpent is also cursed, and a state of enmity is established between the serpent and humankind. However, this enmity is destined to end. It does not establish the permanent domination of Satan over humanity, but reflects a temporary enmity that will end with Satan's defeat.

This text has assumed particular importance in the Christian tradition, which sees in it the *proto-evangelium*—the first proclamation of the good news—in its clear announcement of Satan's defeat: "He will strike at your head, while you strike at his heel." For the most part, Christian tradition has given the text a Marian interpretation based on the Latin version of the text, the Vulgate, which translates the verse with a feminine pronoun ("*She* will crush your head . . ."). However, the pronoun is masculine in the Hebrew text and in the Greek version, the Septuagint. The Jewish tradition is faithful to the Hebrew text and interprets "he" as the Messiah.

For the Man and the Woman

The man and woman are punished, not cursed. As we have seen, the first human *(adam)* came from the earth *(adamah)* and was placed by God in the Garden of Eden, meaning he was elevated to a state superior to his earthly nature. This was the state of grace in which the first humans lived. After the Sin, in Genesis 3:23, the Lord God expelled Adam "from the garden of Eden to till the soil from which he had been taken." In characteristically concrete terms, the sacred author expresses the loss of the state of grace and the supernatural gifts that go along with it: freedom from death and the weaknesses of human nature. Adam will return to the soil *(adamah),* and there he will lead a life confined to his earthly nature.

The relationship between man and woman also reflects the disorder caused by sin. The original equality between them is broken, and the woman becomes subordinate to the man. Work, a natural part of the human condition before sin ("The Lord God took the man and put him in the garden of Eden to till it and keep it," Genesis 2:15), now becomes laborious and painful for him, as childbirth does for the woman.

Nevertheless, the sacred author does not want the story to end with the evil and the punishment. God sends the man and woman out to work the earth (that earth from which they were made—as earthly beings—before being placed in the Garden of Eden), but not without having first clothed them with skins, an expression of divine care even for sinful humankind.

Chapter 14

The Typology of the Account of Original Sin

Jesus and Adam: Antithesis

In the typology of sin there is an exception to the usual rules of typology, in which there is a development from an inferior plane to a superior one, with similarities and differences between the two planes. There cannot be similarities between original sin and redemption; there can only be absolute opposition. As a sinner, Adam is the antithesis of Jesus the redeemer. Jesus restores what Adam ruined.

Already in the Old Testament there is the allusion to a link between Adam and the Messiah.[13] In the temptations that Jesus victoriously faces, we can see the antithesis to the temptations which overcame the first man and woman.[14]

The classic opposition between Adam and Jesus is proposed by Saint Paul (Romans 5:12ff.; 1 Corinthians 15:20ff.). Through Adam death comes to all people, while Jesus brings the resurrection of the dead.

We know that what happens to Jesus happens to every Christian. In Romans 6:3ff., Saint Paul speaks of baptism as our participation in Jesus' death and Resurrection. In other words, it is the sacrament in which we are made to be like Christ who died and has risen. In every person there is a double Adam: the old one through whom everyone dies, and the new one, the redeemed person, born anew through baptism.

This same opposition between Adam the sinner and the Messiah can be found in the patristic tradition. Saint Irenaeus says, "As it was through our first father Adam and because of his disobedience that we were bound to death, it was just, right, and necessary that the yoke of death be broken through the obedience of the One who was made human for our sake."[15]

Tertullian says:

> Why did Christ have to be born from the Virgin? He who was going to consecrate a new order of birth must himself be born after a novel fashion. . . . But the whole of this new birth was prefigured, as was the case in all other instances, in ancient type, the Lord being born as man by a dispensation in which a virgin was the medium. The earth was still in a virgin state, reduced as yet by no human labor, with no seed as yet cast into its furrows, when, as we are told, God made man out of it into a living soul. As then, the first Adam is thus introduced to us, it is a just inference that the second Adam likewise, as the apostle has told us, was formed by God into a quickening spirit out of the ground—in other words, out of a flesh which was unstained as yet by human generation. . . . It was by just the contrary operation that God recovered his own image and likeness, of which he had been robbed by the devil.[16]

In the liturgy we also note the opposition between the wood of the cross and the tree that was the occasion of sin in the Garden of Eden: "For you placed the salvation of the human race on the wood of the Cross, so that, where death arose, life might again spring forth and the evil one, who conquered on a tree, might likewise on a tree be conquered, through Christ our Lord" (Preface of the Exaltation of the Holy Cross).

Mary and Eve: Antithesis

The opposition between *Jesus* and *Adam* is flanked by an antithesis between *Mary* and *Eve*. Thus Tertullian says:

> For it was while Eve was yet a virgin that the ensnaring word had crept into her ear which was to build the edifice of death. Into a virgin's soul, in like manner, must be introduced that Word of God which was to raise the fabric of life; so that what had been reduced to ruin by this sex might by the self-same sex be recovered to salvation. As Eve had believed the serpent, so Mary believed the angel.[17]

The Account of Sin and Parousia

Parousia will bring the complete victory over sin and all its consequences, and the last enemy to be defeated will be death. As Saint Paul
says: "For as all die in Adam, so all will be made alive again in Christ"
(1 Corinthians 15:22). When "God will be all in all," there will no longer
be any place for death or for suffering (Isaiah 25:8); there will only be
room for praise to God (Revelation 5:13).

Chapter 15

The Account of the
Universal Flood

Essential text to be read: Genesis 6:9—9:17

The sin of Adam and the subsequent diminishment of humankind's response to God's salvific invitation signifies a fracture in the plan of God. Evil spreads over the earth. With Cain, humanity is marred by fratricidal blood (Genesis 4:1ff.). The song of Lamech—considered to be one of the oldest biblical texts—shows how violence will no longer have limits (Genesis 4:23–24). Being confronted with the wickedness of humankind, the God of Israel reacts. He pronounces a sentence of condemnation on the evil ones and salvation for the just one, "who was walking with God."

The Literary Genre

The account of the flood is similar in genre to the texts preceding it in the book of Genesis. As with the creation accounts and the account of Sin, we are not dealing with a chronicle of an event as reported by an eyewitness. The tradition of a "universal flood" that almost annihilated life on the earth is widespread among many peoples, including some who are distant from Israel in both time and space. In this we hear the echo of primordial cataclysms, such as the Ice Age. But in the lower parts of Mesopotamia, the setting of the biblical narrative, the discovery of a very deep flood layer beneath which there are still traces of human life suggests a local cataclysm that could correspond to the one recorded in the Bible.

The Babylonian Account of the Flood

A particular Babylonian account of the flood shares many similarities with the biblical account. Here too the sacred author of Genesis might have drawn from the common heritage of tradition, using it as a means to express his particular doctrine, one that reflects an advanced phase in the religious thinking of Israel.

The Babylonian text is the *Epic of Gilgamesh,* already examined in reference to original sin. We will begin with a brief recounting of it, remaining faithful to the principle that biblical texts are formed by the culture from which they arise.

The Babylonian text tells of a cataclysm that the leader of the gods decides to send on the people for no apparent reason in order to exterminate them. Because of the intervention of one god of good will, who does not approve of the decision, one man among all the others is saved. He takes his family and several types of plants and animals into the refuge of a boat that he has constructed according to the god's instructions. Then the flood comes: "And darkness was spread over the earth so that brother could not recognize brother." Even the gods are terrorized: "The gods, like dogs, crouched and were still." The man who escapes the devastation tells how for "seven days and seven nights the wind and flood poured over the earth." Then the flood ceases, and on the seventh day a dove is released from the boat. It flies away but does not find a place to land, and so it returns. Next a crow is sent out. It discovers that the waters have receded, so it eats, splashes about in the water and caws, but does not return to the boat. All the inhabitants of the boat then go out from its four windows. The hero offers a sacrifice by erecting "seven and seven" worship vessels, in which cedar and myrtle are burned. The gods smell the fragrance and gather like flies around the one making the sacrifice.

The points shared with the biblical text are apparent in the corresponding words: the dove, the crow, the Lord who "smelled the pleasing odor" of the sacrifice offered by Noah, who had been saved from the flood (Genesis 8:21). These are popular elements which the author finds in his surroundings and uses word for word in his account; but a deeper examination of the text reveals how common ways of speaking can be used to express a doctrine which is unparalleled in the ancient Middle East.

The Doctrine of the Biblical Account

While there is no specific moral reason for the flood in the Babylonian account, in Genesis the flood is God's punishment of humankind (6:13). Therefore, the first important doctrinal point is that of the morality of the God of Israel, who will not tolerate wickedness. Such a God-concept may seem unimpressive to the modern mind, which is accustomed to a profoundly moral concept of God. However, even a brief look at the Babylonian account reveals how such a concept was altogether counter-cultural in the ancient Middle East. The catastrophe recounted in Genesis is visited upon the world through the will of a personal God whose justice cannot tolerate the spread of wickedness. However, God's justice is accompanied by mercy and loving kindness toward the just one.

The Human Creature

The second doctrinal point pertains to human beings, which the sacred author holds in highest regard. But because the author is a Jew, he cannot conceive of human dignity except in the light of the goodness of God. If maximum respect is demanded for human life, it is because "in his own image God made humankind" (9:6).

The Human Creature and the Nonhuman World

Here also is an expression of the deep and mysterious bond that exists between human beings as earthly creatures and the earth itself. This is the same solidarity we have already observed in the curse on the earth due to Adam's sin. The text describes humankind's conduct with the words "the earth was corrupt; for all flesh had corrupted its ways upon the earth" (Genesis 6:12). The disorder in humankind, for whom creation was made, infects creation itself. The earth seemingly rebels against the one who is the cause of its curse and becomes the instrument of humankind's punishment. Yet, this was not God's intention for the earth in the original created order.

Humankind's behavior seems to have annihilated God's creation. The "waters beneath," which had been divided on the second day of creation, are once again mixed with those "of heaven," and creation is almost returned to the state of chaos. There is no longer anything that has "the breath of life in its nostrils." There is no more life, either animal or human, on the face of the earth.

In this picture of desolation the figure of Noah, the just man, stands out as the only one who guarantees the reestablishment of order because "he walked with God." At the end of the flood the earth is renewed, not only in a material sense, but because all people who will inhabit the earth will be descended from Noah, the just one.

Thus, the work of creation, the very plan of God, will be able to resume its course; the negative element that humankind had introduced into it and that had impeded its development is diminished. God blesses the new inhabitants of the earth with words similar to those with which he blessed the first humans: "Be fruitful, multiply and abound on the earth" (cf. Genesis 9:1ff. and Genesis 1:28ff.). With the world purged of the presence of the wicked, the just one resumes a position in the world analogous to the original condition of Adam. All things are once again placed in his hands. However, while in Genesis 1:28ff. the exercise of humankind's power over the lesser beings appears to be peaceful, after the flood we read about the "fear and dread" that humankind will necessarily arouse in the animals (9:2); their relationship is already one of conflict and struggle.

Furthermore, God promises that the earth will never again rebel against humankind. The regularity of the change of seasons, which God guarantees in Genesis 8:22, is the effect of the renewal of the moral order in humankind and will make the earth a hospitable home for them once again.

The Covenant

The author expresses the new relationship between God and humankind after the flood in terms of a "covenant." This covenant is of cosmic proportions. As in every covenant, there is a gift from God, the assurance of order in nature, and this gift calls for a response, a commitment on the part of humankind: respect for life. Also, there is a mediator of the covenant: Noah, and a sign of the covenant that corresponds to its very nature, an element of the natural world, the rainbow. Like the reference to the sabbath in the account of creation, there is here a projection of the life of Israel onto the cosmic plane, namely that of the covenant between God and humankind, about which we will say more later on.

Numerology

The use of numbers, several of which occur frequently, is a curious element in the account of the flood. The biblical use of numbers is largely symbolic. Throughout the Bible the number 40 indicates a period of waiting and preparation. Moses stayed on Mount Sinai 40 days before receiving the Law. The Jews wandered in the desert 40 years before being able to enter the Promised Land. Jesus stayed in the desert 40 days before beginning his public ministry. Thus, the number 40 always refers to a period of preparation that precedes the realization of highly significant events.

The number 50 (which occurs in the account of the flood in the number 150, 50 times 3) is usually the symbol of a new era. In the fifth day of creation animal life begins. Fifty days after Easter is Pentecost, which for Christians is the fulfillment of Christ's work, and for Jews in the post-biblical tradition is the feast of the gift of the Law, the fulfillment of the Exodus from Egypt. The Hebrew word for the number seven means fullness, completion, perfection.

In conclusion, it is clear from the first pages of the Bible that Israel takes sin very seriously and sees it as a destructive element, not only in the world of human beings but in all of creation. Nevertheless, the biblical message is always a message of hope. In the outbreak of evil there is always a seed that is stronger than destruction, one which is capable of conquering the powers of darkness and evil, a seed from which life can be restored. This message will be further developed in the time of the prophets in the doctrine of the "remnant" that will be for Israel "like dew," an element which sustains and rekindles life.

Chapter 16

The Typology of the Account
of the Universal Flood

As we know, the unity of the divine plan explains and determines the profound analogies between the various moments of its unfolding. In the flood tradition there is the imprint of the mind of God, who is preparing the complete redemption of all people and all things.

Christological Typology: Jesus and Noah

Christological typology sees in Jesus a new Noah; he initiates a renewed humanity.

According to certain interpreters, the dove of Noah prefigured the dove present at Jesus' baptism. In fact, just as in the time of Noah, when through the wood and the water the people received salvation and began a new generation, and when the dove returned to Noah with a sprig of an olive branch, so too it is said that the Holy Spirit descends on the true Noah (Jesus), author of the second generation.[18]

Justin observes: "Noah is saved through the wood of the ark. Jesus saves through the water [of baptism] and the wood of the cross." He then concludes:

> Christ, the firstborn of all creation, has become in a new sense the head of a new race, one which is regenerated by him through water, faith and the wood contained in the mystery of the cross, just as Noah was saved along with his family by the ark which was carried by the waters.[19]

Sacramental Typology: Baptism and the Flood: Purifying Waters

The first letter of Peter describes the sacramental typology of the flood by identifying the flood waters as the prefiguring of baptism, which "now saves you—not as a removal of dirt from the body, but as an appeal to God for a good conscience, through the resurrection of Jesus Christ" (1 Peter 3:21). In the same vein, Tertullian notes:

> For just as after the waters of the deluge, by which the old iniquity was purged—after the baptism, so to say, of the world—a *dove* was the herald which announced to the earth the assuagement of celestial wrath, when she had been sent her way out of the ark, and had returned with the olive branch, a sign which even among the nations is the foretoken of *peace;* so by the selfsame law of heavenly effect, to earth—that is, to our flesh—as it emerges from the font, after its old sins, flies the *dove* of the Holy Spirit, bringing us the peace of God, sent out from the heavens, where is the church, the typified ark.[20]

In the liturgy, the prayer of consecration over the baptismal water says, "The waters of the great flood you made a sign of the waters of baptism that make an end of sin and a new beginning of goodness." In the iconography of the catacombs one frequently finds the figure of Noah stepping forth into a renewed world.

Hence, in a particular way, we live in the Church, the mystery that was already present in germinal form, in the waters of the flood, the waters that purified the world from the presence of the wicked.

Chapter 17

The Account of the Flood and the Parousia

In the account of the flood, we have seen that Israel projects its way of living its relationship with God: the covenant. In Genesis 9:1ff. God offers a perpetual covenant between Himself and the earth and all people, along with all their descendants and "every living thing that is found on the earth." God promises that "the waters shall never again become a flood to destroy all things of the flesh." What God requires in return is the upmost respect for human life, because "in the image of God was humankind made." The sign of restored peace will be the God's "bow in the clouds": the rainbow.

The faithfulness of the Lord's mercy is inscribed in that order in nature which God has promised will never again be disrupted. In the order that regulates the heavens and the earth, human beings can find assurance that God's mercy will never wane.

The prophet Isaiah addresses the theme of the flood and considers it from an eschatological perspective, proclaiming the Lord's word that

> For a brief moment I abandoned you, but with great compassion I will gather you. . . . With everlasting love I will have compassion on you, says the Lord, your Redeemer. This is like the days of Noah to me: Just as I swore that the waters of Noah would never again go over the earth, so I have sworn that I will not be angry with you and will not rebuke you.

> For the mountains may depart and the hills be removed, but my steadfast love shall not depart from you, and my covenant of peace shall not be removed, says the Lord, who has compassion on you. (Isaiah 54:7–10)

The prophet, Zechariah, speaks of Parousia as the time when "the Lord will become king over all the earth; on that day the Lord will be One and his name One" (Zechariah 19:9). There will be no room for anything but the limitless love of God. The prophets educate us to hope.

Chapter 18

Methodological Principles III: The Documentary Theory

"Doublets" in the Bible

Another methodological problem must be addressed, one that becomes more pressing in relation to the historical parts of the Bible, although it is not limited to these parts. The problem of "doublets"—the telling of the same episode more than once and in different ways—now becomes evident. The episode might even be said to occur in two different places and with different characters. In these cases the question of which account correctly reflects history arises. If there are two or more passages that speak of the same event, why are they not given a unified form?

In addition, the texts already considered have contained repetitions and single passages that do not seem to have been written by the same hand. The corresponding solution to this problem, as proposed by various exegetes, points to the so-called "documentary theory" (often referred to as "source criticism"). Among the most prominent of these scholars was Baruch Spinoza (1632–1677), a Portuguese Jew who raised doubts that Moses was the sole author of the Pentateuch. Although this position got him expelled from the synagogue, his books made their way to the reading list of the Catholic Church.

Up until that time the Pentateuch was thought to have been one work written by Moses. Both the Jewish tradition and the gospels speak of it in this way. When one considers the fact that Moses would have had to be the one to describe his own death (Deuteronomy 34), it is clear that at least one part of the Pentateuch in its final draft cannot be attributed to him.

In 1753 the French Catholic doctor Astruc observed that two names are used for God in the Pentateuch: *Elohim* and *Yahweh*. In English these names are rendered *God* and *Lord,* respectively. According to Astruc's theory, the Pentateuch was the result of the combination of two different documents, one whose author used the name *Yahweh*, and another in which the name *Elohim* appears. The two documents were supposedly blended together and drafted by Moses.

The theory was met with great interest. It was then repressed, taken up again, and then further advanced in the hypothesis that there must have been more than two documents involved. This theory was suggested and clarified by the German Protestant exegete Julius Wellhausen, who died in 1918. He distinguished four major documents: Y (Yahwist), E (Elohist), D (Deuteronomist), and P (Priestly Code). Wellhausen also put forth a historical theory, although this part of his work is considered weak. He assigned dates to many of the documents, all after the Babylonian exile in 586 BCE.[21] Further, he relegated to legend many elements that had been considered historical, such as the stories of the patriarchs. The inconsistency of this part of his theory has been demonstrated by archeological studies and by the discovery of extra-biblical texts, which are easily dated as coming from a remote epoch. They confirm the historicity of many elements placed in doubt by Wellhausen, and they refute many of the dates that he proposed.

What can be said today regarding the documentary theory? The subject is still far from being settled. However, it can be affirmed that the documentary theory continues to be foundational in the work of the majority of exegetes. The first edition of *The Jerusalem Bible* came out in 1956; it was the first Bible and the first exegetical work in which one could speak openly, and with the *Imprimatur* (the official approval from the Catholic Church), about the documentary theory. It had been preceded by authoritative documents: the encyclical of Pope Pius XII, *On Promoting Biblical Studies (Divino Afflante Spiritu)* in 1943; the Second Vatican Council Constitution: *On Divine Revelation (Dei Verbum)* in 1965; and the document of the Biblical Pontifical Commission of 1993, to which we have already referred.

Furthermore, one cannot forget that these studies have progressed, along with the recovering of noted and unknown texts (such as those of the Qumran library) and certain archeological excavations (such as Ugarit and Elba), and these studies have not ceased asking the questions and opening up new horizons in biblical research, especially regarding the Pentateuch.

In the United States, W.F. Albright has dedicated himself to passionate research on the relationship between the Bible and the ancient Middle East, particularly focusing on archeological discoveries. In the early 1900s interest was born in a possible cultic origin of several documents, as seen in the biblical theology of von Rad (first edition, 1957). In the Scandinavian school, and mostly tied to the names of H. Gunkel, S. Mowinckel, J. Pedersen, I. Engell, and E. Nielson, there has been a particular focus on the oral tradition, through which many texts certainly passed before taking form in the written word.

From the Oral Tradition to the Written Tradition

Over the course of history, cycles of historically based stories began to be formed about a person (such as the judges or Jacob), a place or a worship site (Bethel, for example). There were multiple renderings of the Law, with further additions as determined by the necessities of life. All of this was preserved in oral tradition and later written down when various threads of tradition were brought together, each presenting a different character.

In current biblical studies, the threads that are most clearly outlined are still those proposed by Wellhausen, of which we offer here only a brief summary while also keeping in mind that what can be said in this field always bears the character of approximation as a working hypothesis.

The *Yahwist* source dates from around the tenth century BCE, more or less to the time of King David. This theological school brings together the scattered traditions into a grand, unified vision that extends from creation to the reign of David.

The *Elohist* source is held to be a little later than the Yahwist and begins its account with the story of Abraham.

The *Deuteronomistic* source is reflected in the book of Deuteronomy, but its spirit has greatly influenced other texts and is particularly reflected in the historical books. It is thought to have originated in the northern kingdom of Israel. Its preaching on the love of God and its strong social concern reflect the development of the great prophetic mission of Israel.

The priestly source is so named because of its prevailing interest in worship and the historical events connected to worship. It conserves material related to worship at the time of Moses or perhaps before him. For the most part, the compilation of this source was done during or after the exile in Babylon, around 586 BCE, when there was a greater sense of urgency to conserve the ancient tradition. It is perhaps the author of this source that directed the final revision of the Pentateuch.

For the most part, those compiling the sources in written form did not blend them together. Rather, they placed the different sources alongside one another and left them intact, even though the sources might have contradicted one another. The existence of doublets in the Bible is a guarantee of the editor's faithfulness to the tradition.

What can be said for now is that various texts were written down in ancient times. Although writing was not yet very widespread, it was common among the Semitic peoples (the first alphabetic text found at Byblos dates to the thirteenth century BCE, not to mention the many earlier, non-alphabetic texts found in Babylonia, Assyria, and upper Syria).

Chapter 19

The Stories of the Patriarchs

With the vocation of Abraham and the election of Israel through the person of the first patriarch, we enter a new phase of the Bible. The first eleven chapters of Genesis recount events of a cosmic character, tackling themes that reach far beyond the borders of Israel. Who made the world? What is humankind's place in the world? Where does evil come from? The answers Israel gives to these questions come from the experience they have already had with God. Even though they might express this experience through the language and mode of speaking common to the peoples of the ancient Middle East, the "spirit" being communicated is radically different.

Beginning with chapter 12 of Genesis, the focus in on the global vision of Israel's history, from a time when they were not yet formed as a people to a time when they would become the people of God. The book of Genesis presents us with the stories of the patriarchs which we could call "a family story."

From a cosmic phase we enter the historical phase of the Bible, and we must first clarify what is intended by the term "history" when we read the Bible.

Biblical Historiography

In compiling history, the sacred author employs different criteria than those of the modern historian. The modern historian searches for details, aiming at reconstructing an event with nearly photographic precision. This type of historical reconstruction is made by researching archives and collecting as much objective data as possible. There are also texts of this sort in the Bible, but the primary intention of the sacred author is the writing of "sacred history," helping us know God through events in which God works. With such an aim, the research of endless details becomes superfluous and the need for precision regarding geographic indications, dates, and names loses much of its importance.

A unique aspect of biblical historiography is its account of the way Israel has experienced certain facts or events in its history, rather than giving a chronicle of facts. In biblical history there is both an account of the events and the interpretation of them.

The Stories of the Patriarchs

The literary genre of the stories of the patriarchs in particular is poetry and popular narration. These stories deal with history but are presented in poetic form and have been passed on for a long period through the oral tradition. Therefore, they are not chronicles according to the modern conception of history but have, above all, a doctrinal aim: They seek to instruct and edify. Their place is in the wider framework of sacred history, which pursues the goal of teaching a specific understanding of God. To this end they adopt criteria and modes of expression that might not correspond to the principles of the modern historian but which are nonetheless effective, primarily in lifting up the religious significance of specific events.

The intention common to all the stories of the patriarchs is primarily to present God as a living Person who is present to His faithful ones, for whom he is guide, helper, and comforter. In view of this general aim, we can recognize particular aims which distinguish various types of stories.

For example, there are stories that seek to explain a geographical phenomenon, such as the story of the destruction of Sodom and Gomorrah (Genesis 18:16ff.). Here the destruction of the region is presented as the result of the condemnation of humankind's immorality.

Other narratives seek to explain the origin of certain sacred places in a divine manifestation, such as Bethel, (Genesis 28:10ff.), Mamre (Genesis 23:11ff.), and Beersheba, a place that is linked both to Isaac (Genesis 26:23ff.) and to Jacob (Genesis 46:1ff.). Stories of this kind are referred to as etiological.

There are also the stories that seek to explain the origin of a name (etymological stories); for example, that of Jacob-Israel (Genesis 32:23ff.).

Chapter 20

The Election of Israel

Israel's Mission

The history of salvation enters a new phase with Abraham. In the first chapters of Genesis we come to know God only through the work of creation. From the moment God chooses Israel in the person of its founder, Abraham, to be his special people, God ties the manifestation of his own self to the history of a people. The history of Israel becomes, in some way, God's history. It is, of course, the "scandal" of the Incarnation: God, who will be manifested in human flesh, is now manifested in the circumstances—at times favorable, at other times adverse—of a small tribe in the ancient Middle East. God entrusts to this small group, whose territory is surrounded by some of the greatest and most powerful nations of antiquity—the Egyptians, the Babylonians, the Assyrians—a particular mission: that of conveying the knowledge of the one God to all people. For centuries, Israel will be unique among the world's nations in knowing that idols are worthless and that the living God is none other than the Lord God of Israel, who created the heavens and the earth.

Yet, Israel's mission is not limited to receiving and transmitting doctrine. As we have said, "sacred history" is an encounter with the living God. Israel is granted a unique experience of God, a personal (even existential) knowledge of the Lord who intervenes in its history and helps "construct" the history together with its people. Israel's mission is not limited to telling people about the ONE God. What Israel transmits to humanity is its encounter with the one God in its own history, which is its very life as the chosen people, the people who live in a special relationship with God.

This particular relationship is initiated on the day the Lord says to Abraham: "Go from your country and your kindred and your father's house to the land I will show you. . . . So Abram went, as the Lord told him" (Genesis 12:1ff.). With these words the dialogue between Israel and God is initiated. God has spoken. The human being has responded by obeying. The dialogue will continue and will engage first the life of the first patriarch and then of his people. In the person of Abraham, Israel takes its first steps as the "priestly people," the people that gives God to others.

The Newness in the Story of Abraham

The vocation of Abraham might seem to be an event that would cause very little commotion in history: a Bedouin wandering from one territory to another. Instead, Abraham's journey will have great repercussions in history. In the person of Abraham, humankind is raised to a different level. The history of salvation comes to a fundamental milestone with the patriarch, and a new dawn of the world unfolds before all people. This dawn will illuminate humankind with a previously unknown light: the knowledge of the living God. One must approach the story of Abraham with the same wonder with which one approaches something altogether new. Everything in the story of Abraham, says Saint Augustine, "breathes the new."

Before such an important fact, one cannot but wonder why God specifically chose the Hebrew people. Why was such a privilege granted to them? Israel must have asked this question as well, and the answer lies in the Bible: The Lord did not choose Israel "because [it was] more numerous than any other people . . . for [it was] the fewest of all peoples. It was because the Lord loved [Israel]" (Deuteronomy 7:7–8). Israel's election is, above all, a gift, a secret of the love of God, a mystery that finds its explanation only in divine charity.

God Chooses the Small

In the distribution of divine gifts one can observe a constant in the Bible: God chooses the small. One has only to leaf through the Bible to realize this. When Gideon is chosen to guide the people, he responds by saying to the heavenly messenger: "My clan is the weakest in Manasseh, and I am the least in my family" (Judges 6:15). When he battles the powerful Midianites, who are threatening Israel, the Lord reduces the number of warriors who will fight by Gideon's side through successive tests, until, "With the three hundred that lapped [the water] I will deliver you, and give the Midianites into your hand" (Judges 7:7).

Not even when Israel is organized as a monarchy will there be deviation from this rule. Like Gideon, when appointed as king, Saul will say to the prophet: "I am only a Benjaminite, from the least of the tribes of Israel, and my family the humblest of all the families of the tribe of Benjamin" (1 Samuel 9:21). Later, when the elderly Samuel is sent to Bethlehem to the house of Jesse in order to anoint the king who will succeed Saul, Jesse brings before him his seven older sons. But only when the youngest, David, arrives does the Lord say to the prophet, "Rise and anoint him; for this is the one" (1 Samuel 16:12).

Because "God's Power Is Revealed in Weakness"

Such a repetitive and consistent occurrence cannot be without a reason. Indeed, it reveals the particular way God works in the history God constructs with the collaboration of humankind. The events narrated in the Bible are the concrete result of the collaborative work of God and humankind both of whom assume their appropriate roles. Yet, in the relationship that is established between God, as "first cause," and humankind in their role as servant, the prevalence of the divine action in the relationship will be far more evident while the role of humankind remains in the shadows and is played by persons of little importance. Had Gideon defeated Midian with a great army, it would have been easy to view his success as a result of the strength of a valiant people. But a victory obtained with three hundred warriors could not be credited to them alone, and therefore gave rise to the question, "Who is the Author of this victory?" Parents would tell their children that God chased away the people "with [his] right hand, and [his] arm," and that "[not] by their own sword did they win the land, nor did their arm give them victory" (Psalm 44:3–4). Thus, Israel learns to put its trust in God alone, and the psalmist, who has learned the lesson of history, says: "For not in my bow do I trust, nor can my sword save me" (Psalm 44:6). Saint Paul will later clarify the principle by saying, "The power of God is revealed in weakness" (2 Corinthians 12:10, paraphrased).[22]

Israel is the human weakness that God chooses to reveal his power. Therefore, a mission unfolds in Israel that is unparalleled in the history of humankind. The prophet Micah (5:7) defines the nature of this mission in this way: Among the many peoples, Israel will be "like dew from the Lord, like showers on the grass, which do not depend upon people or wait for any mortal." The life-sustaining function of dew is essential in a dry country like the land of Israel. Life continues in the dry season solely because of the dews. Even more than the rain, which can be channeled into canals and conserved in cisterns, the dew comes as something that works for humankind's benefit without humankind's participation. It comes purely as a gift from God; people find it in the morning upon awakening, silver and fecund in their fields, and the life-sustaining work has already been done without their even having been aware of it. This is the work for which God chose Israel, and people continue to share in its inheritance, welcoming it as a gift from God.

Chapter 21

Abraham in the History of His Time

ESSENTIAL TEXT TO BE READ: Genesis 12:1—25:11

So great is the religious significance of Abraham—founder of the chosen people of God and the person who first joins the cosmic chorus that will give praise to the ONE God at the completion of history—that his humanity, his being a human among humans, risks being lost in obscurity. Yet in him God has chosen a person like many, a product of his time and his land, rooted in the history and the culture of the ancient Middle East of the second millennium before Christ.

A few modern historians deny the antiquity of the story of Abraham, but the reasons they give are not always convincing. From the Bible we know that Abraham enters Palestine from Ur of the Chaldeans, where the will of the Lord had been shown to him with a precise command: "Go from your country . . ." (Genesis 12:1). He promptly obeys the voice of God and begins his journey, following the Euphrates river to the city of Haran, where his father dies. He then crosses the desert and at last reaches the land of Canaan (later called the Land of Israel.)

Abraham in Canaan

At the time of Abraham the land of Canaan was subdivided into small kingdoms that lived in the orbit of great powers. They were always ready to join forces in order to fight any group among them that would attempt to prevail upon the others (Genesis 14). Abraham, too, finds himself involved in these warlike activities (Genesis 14:12ff.). When his nomadic lifestyle brings him into contact with local chieftains, they sometimes go to Abraham and offer him "good neighbor pacts" (Genesis 21:22ff.).

A Semi-nomadic Life

Abraham is a nomad, or more precisely a semi-nomad. He uses asses rather than the camels used by genuine nomads who are accustomed to traveling long distances. Furthermore, he breeds cattle and goats, which provides him a degree of independence regarding watering spots.

Abraham's stopping places in the Negeb desert, which was completely desolate until the twentieth century and believed to be uninhabitable, gave rise to Wellhausen's theory, mentioned earlier (chapter 18). According to this theory the stories of the patriarchs are primarily legends. However, more recent archeological findings have refuted this theory by uncovering traces of at least 450 water sources there. The fact that the Negeb was habitable is confirmed by the existence of numerous settlements established there today.

Becoming a Settled People

The patriarchs eventually settled down, dividing their activities between raising livestock and cultivating the land, the activity that they slowly dedicated themselves to. The Bible has preserved the detailed account of Abraham's first acquisition of land for Sarah's burial. It is the Israelites' first stable possession in their country (Genesis 23:1ff.).

Among the people of Abraham's world, tribal solidarity runs very deep. Thus, Abraham rushes to the aid of his nephew Lot, who has been taken prisoner (Genesis 14:11ff.), because he is "bone of his bone and flesh of his flesh." In defending his nephew, Abraham is defending himself in some way.

Following the same principle is the custom of intermarriage with members of the same tribe (endogamy). Accordingly, Abraham sends his servant Eliezer to Chaldea to choose a wife for his son Isaac (Genesis 24).

Law in Abraham's Time

The few principles of law that can be gathered from the stories of the patriarchs correspond exactly to what is known of the law of the Middle

East at that time. In purchasing Sarah's burial place (Genesis 23:17), Abraham buys "the field with the cave . . . and all the trees that were in the field." An identical provision is found in Hittite law, establishing the principle that whoever sells a piece of land must sell it with all its plants. Likewise, the fact that the servant adopted as Abraham's son (Genesis 15:2) is deprived of his inheritance rights upon the later birth of Isaac corresponds exactly to a norm contained in the Nuzu Code. According to this code, the adopted son must relinquish every right to the biological heir.

Formal Elements of Religious Life

Even religious life, in which Abraham differs most profoundly from the people of his time, often takes forms similar to those of the ancient Middle East. The covenant with God (Genesis 15:1ff.), discussed later, is celebrated with a sacrifice "in the midst of the halved animals." This is done in accordance with Bedouin custom in which, to ensure the validity of an oath or the faithfulness of a commitment, it was customary to kill some animals, divide them in half, and walk between them. The significance of this practice is not entirely clear. For the most part, it is believed to be a form of oath. Should the agreement be violated, the party reneging on the agreement would share the fate of the sacrificed animals.

Chapter 22

Monotheism

Although Abraham might fulfill all the requirements to be considered an authentic Bedouin of the eighteenth century BCE, there is something that distances and differentiates him from the other people of his time: his faith in the one God.

Monotheistic Intuitions outside Israel

Even prior to Israel there had been some monotheistic stirrings. In the fourteenth century BCE in Egypt, Amenhotep IV expressed his monotheistic faith with an emphasis that still impresses people today. In the seventh century BCE in what is now Iran, the preaching of Zarathustra was substantially monotheistic, and in the fifth century BCE, Sonofane formulated a severe criticism of polytheism in Greece. Sonofane affirmed that there exists one God only, a God who is not at all similar to humankind. He affirmed the existence of a God that sees, feels, and knows all, and who acts by means of thought. With the exception of Amenhotep IV, however, these examples came much later than Abraham and involve the reflections of the intellectually elite. These intuitions remained confined to the person who conceived them, without permeating the religious life of the people.

The Monotheism of the Semitic People

With good reason, scholars are beginning to accept the well-founded theory that the Semitic people were inclined toward monotheism. Nevertheless, this is a monotheism that can be said to be "in process," and one that will be concretized clearly only in the preaching of the prophets, as they affirm the existence of the one God to the exclusion of any other god. It is not until Isaiah that categorical statements of monotheism appear: "Before me no god was formed, nor shall there be any after me. I, I am the Lord, and besides me there is no savior" (Isaiah 43:10–11).

The Monotheism of Israel

Before speaking of monotheism as the existence of one God to the exclusion of any other, one must speak of *henotheism,* the recognition of one God within Israel without excluding the existence of other gods belonging to other peoples. According to the biblical accounts, however, the God of Abraham already reigns alone in the life of the patriarch. God alone cares for Abraham, and God alone receives Abraham's reverence. All of Abraham's life is a colloquy with God, a dialogue in *two* voices: that of the ONE God and that of the person who adores the ONE God only, the living God.

This fact is sufficient to make Abraham—a man of this world, a Bedouin of his time—a figure of outstanding importance in the religious history of humankind and of Israel. Indeed, his faith is not a sudden, sporadic occurrence, a light that shines for a moment and then is extinguished. Rather, it becomes the precious inheritance of the people of Israel, the pivot of Israel's life, the treasure Israel will later share with all peoples.

One cannot but dwell with reverence and gratitude upon the fact that God has made himself known to humankind and that this was realized most fully within the womb of Israel.

Chapter 23

Abraham, Person of the Promise

Every relationship with God is established by means of a gift of God, a gift to which a person responds according to his or her abilities. In the very particular relationship that is established between God and Abraham, the divine gift is a "promise." It is not so much a present gift but a future one, which Abraham awaits with an assurance rooted in the divine promise. For Abraham himself, the gift only begins to be realized; its greater fruits lie in the future. His story unfolds entirely under the sign of hope. In him, Israel begins its history, which involves the future more than the present; it is a history completely based upon waiting, upon expectation.

As Saint Augustine observes, "everything breathes the new" in the story of Abraham. A new vibration moves through history. It is like an electrical charge, provoked by a promise, a charge of hope.

This promise is the connective tissue of the stories of the patriarchs, giving a thematic cohesion to the mosaic of the stories. These stories are varied and sometimes quite profane, but from beneath them—as a seabed current—the saving will of God shines through. For this God, the future holds no secrets, and God occasionally allows human beings a glimpse into that future.

The Two-part Promise

The Lord opens boundless horizons before the eyes of Abraham. The promise that God makes to the patriarch is a dual one: *descendants* as numerous as the stars in the sky through a son who will be wondrously born, and the possession of the *land*. Both of these promises present a double aspect: one that is tied to the present moment and one that will be accomplished only in the future.

Descendants

The birth of Isaac is a great event in the life of Abraham, who is already old, and who has had no offspring by Sarah. Moreover, it is an event that transcends itself, an event that supersedes the limits of the family story: In Isaac all people will be blessed. Undoubtedly, the promise of God is made tangible in this child born from a sterile womb, but it is not limited to him.

The story of Abraham is directed toward something that begins to be realized in his lifetime, but whose greater fruits will ripen only in the future. The birth of Isaac is a great event in the history of salvation, but its greatness lies even more in the future linked to his birth. The present reality, a child, pales in comparison to the future reality that God's word promises: the blessing of all peoples. The full value of the present lies in its containing the seed of the future.

Land

As for the promise of the possession of the land, the Hebrew word used for "land" means "the land of Israel" as well as the land in its entirety. In the texts, one cannot overlook the possibility that the word could have both meanings. In Genesis 13:17, Abraham is given the command to travel through the land—evidently the land of Israel—through its length and breadth so as to take possession of it. But also here we have only a seed of the future reality, the beginnings of a possession that will grow larger. Thus, the land of God is the land of Israel. At the fulfillment of the history of salvation, however, Christ will return to the Father a kingdom that will reach to the ends of the earth (1 Corinthians 15:24ff.).

In the letter to the Hebrews (11:9ff.), it is noted that Abraham resided in the Promised Land as if it did not belong to him. He instead establishes something of a provisional residence, living in tents as will Isaac and Jacob, "as in a foreign land," because he is awaiting that city whose architect and builder is God. Indeed, Abraham's entire life has a transitory, provisional quality that serves to heighten awareness of a future fulfillment.

The Texts

The promise is repeated in several places: Genesis 12:1–3; 13:14–17; 15:4–6; 17:1ff.; 17:16; 22:15ff. The reason for similar duplications in the Bible has already been discussed; nevertheless, it remains possible that the repetition of texts in this case might correspond to repetition of the promise on God's part. Perhaps God was leading Abraham to a gradual comprehension of the promise that was unfolding before him. The particular elements of the various promise texts could be the sign of a divine pedagogy by which God slowly leads Abraham to an always fuller and more profound understanding of what God had told him.

The first communication of the divine promise follows Abraham's call (Genesis 12:1ff.). This text already contains the essential elements of the promise: the assurance of descendants and the indication of Abraham's mission to bring blessing to all people.

In Genesis 13:14–16, God promises Abraham the possession of the land. The text of Genesis 15:1ff. is of great importance because God's promise is followed by Abraham's response: faith.

Genesis 17:1ff. specifies that Abraham will be the father of "a multitude of nations," and that "kings shall come from" Abraham.

In 17:15ff., the promise is repeated with regard to Sarah. She shares with Abraham in the promise and in the blessing.

Genesis 15:6 is linked to Genesis 22:15ff.: Abraham's response of faith to God's word has sustained its greatest test. Therefore, the promise is now solemnly repeated, emphasizing the collaboration of humankind with the work of God: "And by your offspring shall the earth gain blessing for themselves, because you have obeyed my voice" (Genesis 22:18).

The first "servant" chosen by the Lord in the election of Israel responded in a positive way to the invitation he received to collaborate with God in the making of sacred history. Thus history resumes its course charged with a new divine force, shared by humankind.

Chapter 24

Abraham, Father of the Faith

The Response to the Promise: Faith in the Living and Life-giving God

To God's gift of the promise, Abraham responds with faith. What God promises to Abraham is impossible to fulfill for humans. The promise is bound to the life of a child who can be born only because of a particular gift of God. It is not possible to believe God's words without renouncing every human argument concerning the event, without having unlimited trust in God who can bring forth life even in impossible conditions—because God is the Lord of life.

As Saint Paul says, "[Abraham] did not weaken in faith when he considered his own body, which was already as good as dead (for he was about a hundred years old), or when he considered the barrenness of Sarah's womb. No distrust made him waver concerning the promise of God, but he grew strong in his faith as he gave glory to God" (Romans 4:18–20). In the light of Saint Paul's word, Saint Cyril of Jerusalem notes:

> As to his fatherhood, Abraham was physically dead, because he was an old man and, furthermore, was married to Sarah, who was also old. There was no longer any hope of descendants. But God announces to Abraham that he will have them, and Abraham's faith does not break down. Undoubtedly Abraham understood that his body was nothing but a corpse. Nevertheless, he relied not on his physical impotence but on the power of the One who made the promise, because he deemed God worthy of his faith. So the two dead bodies (meaning, two bodies that could not give life)—as one could say—brought a child into the world in a marvelous way.[23]

The Test of Faith

Abraham would have to undergo an even greater test of his faith. In asking for the sacrifice of Isaac (Genesis 22:1ff.), God seems to be canceling the promise, snuffing out the very life that is the first realization of the promise, the first seed from which the "multitude of nations" will receive blessing. Yet, Abraham follows the orders of God without comment, confident, as it says in Hebrews 11:17ff., "that God is able even to raise someone from the dead—and figuratively speaking, he did receive [Isaac] back."

Referring to this text, Saint Cyril continues: "He offered to God his only son, believing that God can raise the dead. He sacrificed him in his heart [in his intentions], but through the goodness of God, he was given back his son alive."[24] Isaac is dead in the intentions of his father, who does not hesitate in his obedience to God. It seems to Abraham that his son has died and risen. It is as though he has received the gift of Isaac's life twice.

Therefore, we can specify the object of Abraham's faith: It is already the antithesis between life and death, which will constitute the core of the paschal mystery. Abraham believes God to be the giver and the Lord of life, the one who gives life, can take it away, and give it back again. Commenting on the seeming contradiction that the pronoun "we" seems to imply when Abraham says to his servants, "We [meaning himself and Isaac] will come back to you" (Genesis 22:5) after making sacrifice, Origen says,

> "We will come back to you." Abraham, are you not willing to sacrifice him, or do you lie to us? Abraham answers: "I do not lie; it is the truth. I want to and I must sacrifice my son, just as it is also true that we will return, because I believe. I believe that which God has promised cannot but be fulfilled. How it will happen, I do not know, but God is even capable of raising the dead."[25]

The Faith of Abraham and the Faith of the Christian

The object of Abraham's faith is, therefore, the same as the object of our faith, which is founded on the resurrection of the Christ and affirms the possibility of every person reaching resurrection "through him, with him and in him."

Though substantially the same, the faith of Abraham and the faith of the Christian differ in their degree of clarity and precision. The faith of Abraham is projected completely toward the future, while the faith of the Christian is based on an event that has already been realized—and is therefore already operative—but which is also awaiting its final fulfillment.

Like Abraham, Christians believe in God as the giver of life. Abraham is called, rightly so, the "father of our faith." We are joined to him by faith in the same God and by the same hope. The resurrection of Christ is rooted in the great test of Abraham's faith. Also, the "type" is present in the future events in some way, because it already contains the seed. The seed of the faith of every Christian is found in the faith of Abraham. When Abraham climbs Mount Moriah to sacrifice Isaac, the dawn of that faith breaks through. The same faith will reach its "noon" on the day of Easter, when it becomes possible to say, "The Lord is truly risen!"

Life-giving Faith

Faith in God as the giver of life is the wellspring of life. When God's promise meets with Abraham's faith, the spark of life springs forth. Abraham's faith opens the door so that God's power can work in him through his recognition of his incapacities and his confession of the goodness and power of God. Thus, Abraham's faith is a faith that welcomes the gift of God with humility and awareness.

In fact, every act of faith is composed of two moments. The first is negative: the recognition of human insufficiency. The other is positive: trust in the Person in whom one believes, and thus reverence in response to that Person's goodness and power. Conscious of his inability to father a child, Abraham relies on God alone, and his physical sterility is transformed into the ability to beget a son. In his son Isaac, Abraham could see with his own eyes, thus in a concrete way, the power of the life-giving God who had worked through his sterility. Faith had allowed the divine blessing to unfold its life-giving work in him. This faith gave life that humankind could never have given. What Abraham fathered was not born because of his own doing but because of the blessing that faith had welcomed. Thus, Abraham might have said with Saint Paul, "I can do all things through him who strengthens me" (Philippians 4:13).

Chapter 25

The Covenant[26]

When God's gift is met with Abraham's response, a particular bond is established between them, a bond that is usually called a *covenant, pact,* or *testament.*

Although *covenant* is the more commonly used term, *testament* is perhaps preferable to the terms *pact* and *covenant,* both of which imply equality between the two parties. For this reason they are less accurate in expressing the relationship between God and humankind, which is an unequal one. *Testament* stresses that the one who benefits does so solely because of the goodness of the testator and not because of his own merits.

The terms *pact* and *covenant* point to a relationship that is not biological nor a given fact as is the relationship between parents and their offspring. Such a relationship does not require an agreement but is already established naturally. *Pact* and *covenant* indicate an act of the will, a free choice resulting in a bond that did not previously exist. In our use of the word, *covenant* indicates a free choice on God's part, as well as a free choice on the part of human beings, who accept the gift of God.

To my knowledge, the concept of a covenant between God and humankind is a unique reality in the history of religions. In certain ancient Middle Eastern texts there are allusions to pacts with some deities, but they are pacts of limited importance, tied to particular situations. In Israel, the covenant with the Lord affects the whole life of the whole people.

The Preferential Love of God for Israel

Because of the covenant, God loves Israel with a preferential love (in Hebrew, *hesed*). Israel has become God's special possession. A relationship of benevolence toward humankind is thus established, a relationship that is constant on God's part, although humankind sometimes proves unworthy of it. This does not mean God's part of the covenant is altered or diminished, for "the gifts and the calling of God are irrevocable" (Romans 11:29). The sinner knows he or she can call on God, saying, "Have mercy on me, O God, according to your steadfast love *(hesed)*" (Psalm 51:1). Accordingly, God says, "I have loved you with an everlasting love" (Jeremiah 31:3).

The Rite of the Pact

The bond that is established through the meeting of God's gift with humankind's response is celebrated through a rite. We have already referred to the rite that ratifies the covenant between God and Abraham (Genesis 15:17–21) and to its background as worship.

After completing the act of worship prescribed by the Lord, Abraham falls into a deep sleep, and "a smoking firepot [appeared] and a flaming torch passed between [the] pieces" of the slain animals.

The deep sleep *(tardemah)* mentioned here indicates Abraham's state of passivity, of complete surrender to the presence of God at work. This presence appears in the form of a flame darting between the halves of the slain animals, signifying the participation of the divine in the celebration. The deep sleep of Abraham and the flaming presence of God are meant to represent the respective roles of the two parties: God who works and the human being who lets go so that God can work.

The Sign of the Pact

The covenant celebrated in the rite is not restricted to the person who mediates it, but is meant to last through time. Hence, there arises the need for a sign that distinguishes all those who participate in the covenant and reminds each one of God's promise to Abraham. Circumcision is the sign of the covenant made between God and Abraham (Genesis 17:9ff.). Every male Jew carries in his flesh the sign that signifies his participation in the bond that joins Israel with God.

The Characteristics of the Covenant

For God's part, this new bond is based on a promise, which gives the bond a particular character. The covenant with Abraham, as we have already said, is composed more of expectation and longing toward a future fulfillment than of enjoying a present reality. The covenant carries within itself an urgent need for fulfillment. It is characterized by its universality ("In you all people will be blessed"), but its universality is a potential one whose seed is stored in a small group of Bedouin nomads. The faith of Abraham is faith in the God who raises the dead, even though Isaac only approaches death. The Lord's covenant with Abraham presents the characteristics of something that is not complete in itself. Just as Abraham left for a land known only to God, so history moves toward a destination unknown except to God alone; yet, with providential love, God both knows and prepares these destinations.

Chapter 26

The Typology of the Story of Abraham

The typology of the story of Abraham is so vast that discussion of it must be limited. The liturgy of the Church frequently presents the figure of Abraham as the founder of the faith, the person in whom is realized the first fruits of the life of faith we now live. There are frequent allusions to a first fulfillment of the promise made to Abraham in Christ. The Magnificat proclaims: "He has helped his servant Israel, in remembrance of his mercy, according to the promise he made to our ancestors, to Abraham and to his descendants forever" (Luke 1:54–55). In the Benedictus, Zechariah says, "Blessed be the Lord God of Israel, for he has looked favorably on his people and redeemed them. . . . [he] has remembered his holy covenant, the oath he swore to our ancestor Abraham" (Luke 1:68ff.). In the offertory of the funeral Mass of the Missal of Pius V are the words: "Saint Michael, carry the souls up to the holy light as you once promised to Abraham and to his descendants."

Christological and Sacramental Typology

The typological themes pertaining to Christ and the sacraments are discussed together here because the typology of the story of Abraham relates to the figure of Christ in his essential roles as victim and priest. The first aspect is to be found in Isaac, the second in Melchizedek.

Jesus and Isaac: The Sacrifice

Regarding the imagery of victim, Saint John Chrysostom writes,

It was necessary that the truth be outlined and prepared in the shadows: there an only child, here an Only Child; there a beloved one, here a Beloved One. The former is offered by the father as sacrifice, while the latter is delivered up by the Father: The spiritual Lamb is offered for the world, to free people and bring them to the truth.

The comparison of Abraham with God the Father is also found in the writings of Saint Irenaeus, among others.

The comparison between Isaac and Jesus as victims is further stressed by Tertullian, who goes into great detail:

Among the figures of the passion there is, first of all, Isaac, who, when he was to be delivered up by the father, carried the wood himself. There is designated already then the death of Christ who was given up as victim by the Father and who carried the wood of the passion himself.

Saint Augustine extends the comparison to other particular points: "Isaac obeys God, makes a journey of three days, sends the servants away, and carries the wood on his shoulders." The analogy to Jesus is evident: He is obedience to the will of the Father personified; he stayed three days in the tomb, suffered the abandonment of the disciples, and carried the wood of the cross on his shoulders.

The relationship between Isaac and Jesus is echoed in the liturgy. The second reading of the Easter Vigil is taken from Genesis 22—the narrative of the sacrifice of Isaac. This liturgical context points to the link between Isaac's coming down from the mountain alive and Christ's glorious resurrection.

In a manner of speaking, the "protagonist" in both of these incidents is faith in God, placing total trust in a God who is "able even to raise someone from the dead" (Hebrews 11:11ff.). It is for this reason that Abraham is called "the father of our faith."

Jesus and Melchizedek: The Priesthood

In Eucharistic Prayer I, also called the Roman Canon, the sacrifice of Isaac is mentioned alongside those of Abel and Melchizedek. In the Christian tradition, these three sacrifices are constantly compared. All three are often represented in the most ancient depictions in the catacombs (for example, in the Roman catacombs of Saint Priscilla and Saint Domitilla). Such images were never made for merely decorative purposes, but always had underlying doctrinal and theological concerns. Thus, they are very important documents of the tradition. The depiction of the sacrifices of Abel, Isaac, and Melchizedek on the walls of the catacombs and basilicas (for example, in the new Saint Apollinaris Church in Ravenna) was meant to express the "golden thread" that unites the various forms of offering to God throughout history.

The priestly role of Jesus is anticipated in the person of Melchizedek, to whom Jesus is mysteriously linked. We read in the letter to the Hebrews (7:1ff.),

> This "King Melchizedek of Salem [was] a priest of the Most High." . . . His name, in the first place means, "king of righteousness"; next, he is also king of Salem, that is, "king of peace." Without father, without mother, without genealogy, having neither beginning of days nor end of life, but resembling the Son of God, he remains a priest forever.

The author of Hebrews observes that Melchizedek is an isolated figure whose genealogy is not delineated—an extraordinary fact in the Bible, in which the name of the father at least is indicated—and whose life story is unknown apart from the brief episode recorded for our remembrance of him. From these facts, some deductions have been made which Saint Ambrose explains:

> Who is Melchizedek? "Without a father"—it was said—"and without a mother, without ancestry, and his life has no beginning or ending." So it is written in the letter to the Hebrews. "Without father or mother," it is said, similar to whom? To the Son of God. The Son of God was born without a mother as far as his "heavenly" ancestry is concerned, because he was born only from God the Father. And, on the other hand, he was born without a father when he is born of the Virgin, because he was not conceived by virile seed, but he was conceived by the Holy Spirit and born of the Virgin Mary, coming forth from a virgin womb. Alike in all ways to the Son of God, Melchizedek was also a priest, because Christ is also a priest, and of him it is said: "You are a priest forever, according to the order of Melchizedek."[27]

Chapter 27

The Story of Abraham and the Parousia

As we have seen, the story of Abraham carries within itself an urgent need for fulfillment, which will be realized throughout the various stages of history—the Exodus, redemption in Christ—but which will be entirely fulfilled only at the Parousia. The story of Abraham, which we can define as a "family story," presses on toward universality. This universality has not yet been reached, either in the Exodus—the event by which the Israelites are formed into a people set apart by God from all other peoples on earth—or in the establishment of the Church, which for now is only potentially universal; although she opens her doors to all people, not everyone crosses the threshold.

The Multitude of Peoples in Jerusalem

The descendants of Abraham have not yet brought the richness of their blessing to all people. However, the prophets tell us about "that day" on which the multitude of peoples will flock to Jerusalem to worship the living God (Isaiah 60:1ff.), and they describe for us the heavenly Jerusalem, the place all people will inhabit when the kingdom of God has reached its final and permanent phase (Isaiah 54:1ff.; 60:10ff.).

From an eschatological perspective, we find here once more the two elements of the promise made to Abraham: descendants as numerous as the stars in the sky and the possession of the land.

The elements outlined in the prophetic texts are taken up again in Revelation 21:1ff., where the author says: "Then I saw a new heaven and a new earth" and goes on to describe the new Jerusalem, which comes down from heaven in the midst of the people. Furthermore, in Revelation 5:1ff., the descendants of Abraham are found gathered around the Lamb worshiping him forever. Is there a link between "the Lamb who was slain," the one who was declared worthy to receive honor, glory, and praise, and the ram which takes the place of Isaac on Mount Moriah? Can we detect the "golden thread" that binds them together?

Chapter 28

Moses and the History of His Time

ESSENTIAL TEXTS TO BE READ: Exodus 1:1–21, 24:1–18; Numbers 9—23, 20:1–28; Deuteronomy 31:1—34:12

Since the call of Abraham, the people had been walking along the pathway of history for approximately half a millennium when another servant figure, Moses, rose up to mark another milestone in the divine plan.

If everything was embryonic with Abraham, with Moses everything is more definite and organized. The Hebrew people, who had been a conglomeration of nomadic tribes, are now formed into a people that finds its connective fabric in the Torah, the expression of the will of the God of Israel. The presence of the Lord, which was sporadic in the time of the patriarchs, now becomes stable and concrete in the cloud that guides the people in the desert. Later, the Ark of the Covenant will serve the same function. Furthermore, the function of Abraham as mediator is now designated to the "priestly people."

Previous chapters have briefly traced the movement of Abraham, first from Ur of Chaldea and then to Palestinian soil, according to the laws of seasonal migration. Later, as we have been able to detect there are signs of the patriarchs having begun to live a sedentary life in the Holy Land and making their earliest attempts at farming (Genesis 27:27ff.). By the time of Moses, Israel is in Egypt.

The fertility of the Nile Valley was a great attraction for inhabitants of less fertile lands, and in times of famine it was a place to escape for newer and less experienced farmers. Hence, there was a constant movement of people to Egypt, and the Jews numbered among these people

(Genesis 12:10ff., 42:1ff., 43:1ff.). Such an influx of immigrants had a two-fold effect: Hordes of hungry people flow into the land, but among them are skilled people who then often obtain key positions in the country receiving them. (This is seen in the story of Joseph, Genesis 39:1ff.)

The Exodus and the Sea Peoples

Because of such movement of people, Israel was residing in Egypt at the time of Moses. But the Exodus of the Hebrew people must be considered in the context of a vast movement of peoples that upsets the Middle East between 1300 and 1200, BCE. During this period there was an invasion of the so-called "sea peoples," originating in the north, who arrive at the threshold of Egypt and weaken the country, thus making the departure of the Hebrew people possible. The Philistines settle among these sea peoples along the Mediterranean coast, and in doing so make it impossible for the Hebrew people to reach the land of Israel by following the shortest route. They are forced to wander in the Sinai Peninsula for a long period of time.

The Exodus is thought to have occurred under the Pharaoh Menaphtah (1224–1214 BCE); the pharaoh who oppressed the Jews would have been his predecessor, Rameses II (1290–1224 BCE). These dates concur with archeological evidence. On the basis of these dates it is possible to verify the existence of a culture that existed on Palestinian soil during that time, one which carried traces of the recent beginnings of an agrarian lifestyle, such as primitive architecture and a lack of goods for trade.

The Sources

The events of the Exodus up to the arrival of the Hebrew people in the Promised Land are recorded in the books of Exodus, Numbers, and Deuteronomy. The first two of these books have a more specifically narrative character, while the third continues the historical narrative as an object of meditation and exhortation with a style that presages that of the prophets.

God's History

These books record the many changes—sometimes dramatic, sometimes favorable—that accompany this part of Israel's history. We see God intervening in the history of his people, directing them toward a specific goal. Indeed, the story of the Exodus has a precise orientation: the liberation from slavery points toward the gift of the Torah, which binds the people of God together. The Torah creates a new relationship between the Lord and his people. This relationship is concretized in a new presence of God in the midst of his people and then in the organization of worship.

This is the time when Israel painstakingly takes its first steps toward the freedom of the children of God, although the people of Israel sometimes bemoan the loss of the material abundance they possessed during their time of slavery, and in doing so provoke God's anger. But between the wrath of God and the people stands Moses, intervening with his prayers even to the point of asking that he be erased from the "book of life" if in so doing Israel might be saved.

The People's History

The story of the Exodus is both the history of God and the history of the people. The divine plan of salvation is realized in this history, and thus we can catch a glimpse of the Lord's will, which guides it like a thread binding together the whole. At the same time, the entirely human actions and decisions provide a firsthand view of God's people as "flesh and blood," experiencing all the weaknesses and difficulties shared by everybody in this world.

In the desert Israel encounters all the expected difficulties: thirst (Exodus 15:22ff.; 17:1ff.) and hunger (Exodus 16:1ff.), the need to find water in order to set up camp (Exodus 15:27), and the hostility of the people in the lands through which Israel passes. The settled people do not look favorably upon a horde of nomads in the middle of their cultivated fields, and they are ready to resist Israel in armed combat. Confrontations of this sort cause the Israelites to make some long detours, which greatly prolong their sojourn in the desert (Numbers

20:14ff.). At other times, however, they accept the challenge and fight for the right to pass through the land (Numbers 21:21ff.).

Sometimes the Israelites are ambushed, as by the Amalekites (Exodus 17:8–16). Moreover, they are not without the internal difficulties that arise from fatigue and weakness. On these occasions they complain, "Weren't there sufficient burial places in Egypt? Why did we have to come to this desert to die?" At times, because of ill will and lack of faith, certain people try to stir up the others, describing the Promised Land as one full of entrapments and dangers and calling on the people to doubt Moses (Numbers 14:1ff.). Dathan and Abiram object to Moses' particular role, affirming the equality of all the chosen people before the Lord: "You have gone too far! All the congregation are holy, every one of them, and the Lord is among them. So why then do you exalt yourselves above the assembly of the Lord?" (Numbers 16:1ff.).

The Figure of Moses

Against this backdrop, Moses stands out as a true spiritual giant, always depending on the help of the Lord, which was promised to him at his calling: "I will be with you" (Exodus 3:1ff.). The help of the Lord empowers a man who is weak and timid by himself. At his calling, Moses tries to avoid God's summons by alleging to have a speech impediment. But God is not so easily refused; God tells Moses that his brother Aaron will serve as spokesman (Exodus 4:15).

Moses bears all the burdens of the people, but not without sometimes bitterly complaining to the Lord: "Did I conceive all this people? Did I give birth to them, that you should say to me, 'Carry them in your bosom, as a nurse carries a sucking child,' to the land that you promised on oath to their ancestors?" He even goes so far as to say, "If this is the way you are going to treat me, put me to death at once," because the task given to him is so burdensome (Numbers 11:12–15).

Moses is also a person of flesh and blood. Intertwined in him are weakness and strength: the weakness of the human being and the strength of God, such that Moses can be said to be the greatest prophet in Israel. The Lord spoke with him "face to face" (Deuteronomy 34:10; Exodus 33:11).

Chapter 29

Exodus and Passover

The Exodus occurs as a dramatic struggle between life and death. Death hangs threateningly over Egypt. "Toward midnight" every Egyptian family mourns its firstborn, "for there was no house without its dead." But death passes over the Israelites and does not touch them, for they are protected and saved by the blood of the lamb. At last, urged to depart by the Egyptians who said, "Otherwise we shall all be dead," the Israelites reach the shores of the Red Sea. There death threatens them again, but again it is thwarted. Because of a strong easterly wind, the waters separate and a way is cleared for them to pass through unharmed, while the waters swallow up the Egyptians: "The floods covered them, they went down into the depths like a stone" (Exodus 15:5). The very same waters that part miraculously and save the Israelites now bring death to the Egyptians.

The Encounter with God in the Exodus

The Israelites sing, "Your right hand, O Lord, glorious in power—your right hand, O Lord, shattered the enemy" (Exodus 15:6), when they have reassembled, unharmed, on the other shore. Israel now experiences one of its great encounters with God, an encounter that the prophets call the great meeting of love between the Lord and his people. The Lord meets Israel in the desert as if it is an abandoned child: "Then I saw you as I was passing. Your time had come, the time for love." God claims Israel as his own, adorns it with jewels and transforms it (Ezekiel 16:1ff.). The God Israel encounters is the God of Abraham, Isaac, and Jacob, the same God who saves from death and who is the master of life. Just as the highest moment of Abraham's life was marked by the contrast between death and life, so also, when Israel experiences the pivotal moment of its history, there is once again the mystery of death and life, a mystery of richer life being born from death.

Having passed through the Red Sea, Israel can rightly be considered a different people. A page of its history has been closed forever—that of its subjugation to an idolatrous people—and, on the other shore of the sea, Israel now shows its new face, the face of the liberated people of God. The waters separate Israel from a past that will never return, and then open up before the people a new history. It is as though, in the very moment Israel emerges from the waters of the Red Sea, it is born to a new life.

The Exodus is a pivotal event in the history of the Jews and in the history of salvation. It is the first realization of the promise made to Abraham: The people of God have at last been born and are on their way to the land which the Lord pledged to give them.

As the vital core of both the national and religious life of Israel, the Exodus is the constant focus of Jewish catechesis, in which parents remind their children of the Lord's great deeds on behalf of his people. But the children of future generations must not merely *know* what God has done. The encounter with God does not consist in merely being aware of God's actions; rather, the people must also *live* that history so that it will be renewed in each of them. Every Jew must be able to participate in the liberation and salvation that the Lord has given as a gift to Israel. The Passover rite renders the Exodus event present for each Jew; it offers to everyone, in every generation, the possibility of actually participating in the Exodus.

The Passover Liturgy

The liturgical prescriptions regarding Passover are found in Leviticus 23:4ff., Exodus 12:25ff. and 13:5ff., and Deuteronomy 16:1ff. These texts reveal Passover's progressive development, as well as the various cultural strata that compose it.

The liturgical structure of the Jewish Passover comes from the overlaying of three different cultural strata, as the three essential elements of the rite—the paschal lamb, the unleavened bread, and the bitter herbs—indicate. The paschal lamb comes from an essentially pastoral civilization, in which the produce of the flocks is offered to the deity. It reflects the nomadic period of the history of the Jewish people.

The bitter herbs and the unleavened bread reflect an agricultural civilization, the kind the Jews establish upon entering the land of Canaan. In most agricultural civilizations, there are festivities at the beginning of spring designed to celebrate the beginning of the harvest, and thus the recovery of life in nature. Such festivities are intended to signify a distinct break between the winter period, in which nature sleeps as if dead, and springtime, in which nature reawakens. These festivities are made up of rites and customs that seek to bring closure to the season that is ending—a period of death—and at the same time signify that everything is now new, devoid of the elements of death. The intention of the celebration is to break all continuity between the two periods, because the first period can bring into the second seeds of death. All must begin *ex nova*.

In this vein, the custom of putting out the fire and re-lighting it comes to mind. This custom, which had great significance among those peoples who kept fire constantly burning, is still reflected in our Easter liturgy. The custom of eating only unleavened bread, bread which is completely new, is a custom of this kind. It is not made of yesterday's yeast and therefore is not connected to the past. Furthermore, the bitter herbs are an emetic (an agent that induces vomiting) and thus express in an ingenuous and primitive way the desire for interior cleansing and renewal.

Traces of the naturalistic background of Passover are found in Leviticus 23:10ff., which prescribes the offering of the first sheaf of the spring harvest to the Lord.

The Purely Jewish Characteristics

To these two strata in the Passover, there is added a third that is strictly Jewish, documented in the texts of Exodus and Deuteronomy: the historical interpretation of the elements mentioned—that is, their being placed in relationship to the Lord's work in the Exodus event. There remain in the Passover those elements which Israel absorbs from other peoples, but here they are "God-fashioned." They no longer refer to the impersonal, generative power of nature, but to the Lord himself, who guides history. Therefore, the lamb is what saves the Israelites from the angel of death that passed over Egypt, the bitter herbs are a remembrance of the bitter experiences of the Jews as slaves, and the bread is unleavened because there was no time to let it rise at the moment of the Exodus. Thus, the three paschal elements lose their naturalistic character and are connected to precise historical facts.

The religion of Israel is a historical religion, which means that God is known not merely through the contemplation of nature, but primarily through the work he does in history for his people. This is the particularity first of Judaism and then of Christianity. The naturalistic component becomes secondary in importance to the personal relationship between the Lord and Israel. The Gentiles might recognize God in the forces of nature, but Israel has a particular experience of God that is more intimate and more profound. For Israel, God is a person, imminent, caring and guiding, who has said: "You will be my people, and I will be your God." Israel is the special possession of the Lord, and the Lord is the God of Israel in a particular way.

Through the Passover rite, every Jew, even today, relives the Exodus drama of death and life, while at the same time asking that "the Messiah come soon in our day."

Chapter 30

The Gift of the Law

The Importance of the Torah

The Exodus from Egypt finds its completion in the gift of the Torah. In fact, Jewish tradition speaks of the "engagement" between the Lord and Israel at the Red Sea, and of their "marriage" at Mount Sinai. The freedom that is given to the Jews in the flight from Egypt is a freedom to better serve God. The Torah constitutes Israel as the people of God, cementing the union between Israelite and Israelite and between all of Israel with God. It is in the Law that Israel finds its *ubi consistam,* the reason for its existence. The people of God, whom the Lord had chosen in the person of "father Abraham," had had enough experience of the living God to be capable of receiving the Torah.

The term "law" in biblical language does not have the judicial connotation that it has in our language. Law (in Hebrew: *torah*) means "teaching"; therefore, it is the expression of the wisdom of God who, after having made himself known as One, now reveals himself as a liberator on both the political and spiritual levels. To this end, God teaches Israel how to walk in his ways, by giving them the Torah. We can understand why Judaism exalts the Torah as such a great gift of God. The psalmist longs to meditate on it day and night, because it is "a lamp to my feet and a light to my path" (Psalm 119:105). God, in his goodness, has lighted the pathway of humankind so that they need not stray to the right nor to the left, but can go straight toward him.

The Feast of the Torah: Pentecost

Just as Passover celebrates the exit of the Jews from Egypt, Pentecost celebrates the gift of the Law. All of Israel, says Jewish tradition, was present at Mount Sinai at the moment the Torah was given to Israel, both present and future generations, because absence in that moment would have indicated separation from one's own people. Hence, it is necessary to offer every Israelite participation in God's great gift through the rite. The feast of Pentecost in the biblical texts (Leviticus 23:15ff.; Deuteronomy 16:9ff.) retains a clearly agricultural character: It is the feast that concludes the spring harvest. The historicizing process spoken of in reference to Passover is applied to Pentecost in the post-biblical period. The synagogue prescribes the reading of the account of the Mount Sinai experience for the feast of Pentecost (Exodus 19), thus transforming the nature of the feast and tying it definitively to the gift of the Torah.

Casuistic Laws and Apodictic Laws

In the study of the Bible, it is necessary to distinguish between casuistic laws, which present a particular case and prescribe the relative manner in which one is to conduct oneself (for example, in Exodus 21:23), and apodictic laws (from the Greek *apodeiknumi:* to declare, proclaim), which are absolute norms that exclude the consideration of particular cases.

In this vein, the principle stated in regard to literary genres applies: There are many casuistic laws that Israel has in common with other ancient Middle Eastern peoples. These laws can be compared to and better understood in light of the Babylonian codes and Hittite codes, among others.

The Eminence of the Decalogue

A very special place is reserved for the Decalogue, the Ten Commandments, of which the Bible has preserved two versions: Exodus 20:1ff. and Deuteronomy 5:1ff. The Decalogue is clearly superior to any other ancient code. Even today, and rightly so, it is the foundation of every moral code.

The Decalogue enunciates certain absolute principles ("You shall not kill," for example), thus looking beyond specific cases. This is a milestone in the development of the human conscience, which has achieved the maturity of the adult mind with the Decalogue: the adult mind does not stay only with particulars but arrives at abstraction.

Obedience Motivated by Love

The Decalogue is the codification of the natural law, the law written in the conscience of each individual, the law that makes communal life possible for human beings. But both versions of the Decalogue begin with a religious character: the Lord who gives the Law is the same God that brought Israel out of Egypt, out of the house of bondage. Before knowing the rules, it is essential to know the one prescribing them. Before knowing what one must do, it is necessary to know *for whom* one does it. Before being about adherence to rules, moral life is about the establishment of relationship. In this case, the relationship is with that God who "has brought (Israel) out from the land of Egypt, out of the house of slavery" (Exodus 20:2; Deuteronomy 5:6).

One could say it is this act of God which gives birth to Israel as a free people. "When Israel was a child, I loved him . . . I taught Ephraim to walk, I took him up in my arms," says the prophet Hosea (Hosea 11:1ff.). Israel had to learn to walk in such a way as to measure up to the freedom which it had received as a gift.

The Torah is God's gift of love. The people's observance of it is born from their relationship with the God who "brings out," the God who liberates. Their observance of the Torah is a result of that relationship. And that is why Israel speaks of the Torah as a gift, and why the entire Psalm 119 sings its praises.

The Decalogue goes on to specify that God punishes the wicked up to the third and fourth generation and shows mercy to those who love him up to the thousandth generation. Thus, it is explicitly stated that the Lord's mercy prevails over his severity. In a code of law this could be misconstrued as nonsense if it did not signify that the Lord demands an obedience that is rooted in love. The obedience God desires from humankind must not be the fruit of fear. God has chosen Israel as his "servant" so that it may freely collaborate with him in the plan of salvation, not merely obey him as a frightened slave.

The Sins of Desire

The Decalogue also takes into consideration the sins of desire, a fact of utmost importance. The value of an action does not rest so much in its execution or lack thereof, but in the heart's intention. It is not only the external action that can be offensive, but also the interior action that might escape human control, but which cannot escape the loving and vigilant "jealousy" of a God who "scrutinizes the loins and the heart."

Here, the pathway is opened for the preaching of the prophets, who will emphasize the need for one's actions to be accompanied by right intention. They will say that sacrifices are acceptable to the Lord only if offered by clean hands (Isaiah 1:1ff.). The Decalogue is the beginning of a morality that is progressively deepened through the prophets. The Jewish tradition will strongly emphasize the importance of interior attitude *(kawanah)* in the doing of works. In proclaiming that the poor, the meek and the peacemakers are "blessed," the gospel focuses not merely on the individual fleeting act, but on the constant attitude of the heart.

Chapter 31

The Law and the Spirit

The Torah as Indicator of Sin

Since Judaism rightly holds the Torah in high esteem, the vehement argument against the Law in the letter to the Romans (7:1ff.) is astonishing at first glance. Saint Paul seems to view the Torah negatively when he states, "If it had not been for the Law, I would not have known sin" (7:7) and, "When the commandment came, sin revived" (7:9). In view of these statements, the apostle seems to contradict himself later when he says that "the Law is holy, and the commandment is holy and just and good" (7:12).

A more careful examination of the text, however, reveals how Saint Paul's thinking follows that of the psalmist, who spoke of the Torah as a lamp at the feet of the pious person and a light on his or her path. If the Law is light, it is a guide that illumines the path to be followed, but at the same time it reveals the dangers hidden in the darkness. That is why Saint Paul can say he would not have known sin if it were not for the existence of the Law. No one claims that there is something negative in the light itself, even though it can sometimes point to ugliness. Ugliness is negative; there is nothing negative about the light itself. The Law has the task of being our indicator, our teacher, or, as Galatians 3:24 says, "our guardian." Because the Law points out sin—a positive task—the Law is sacred. But it cannot defeat sin. Its task is limited: It reveals sin but does not heal it; it shows the way but does not help one follow it.

The Law as an External Bond

Saint Paul does not refer to the Decalogue specifically in his argument, but to the law in general, which he understands as a commandment that binds humankind together in an external way.

Much has been written on this text, some of which seeks to divide the law of the Old Testament and that of the New Testament. But the gospel is *not* a new law but a new Person, the Person of Christ, who in himself establishes a new relationship between God and humanity. Therefore, he makes it possible for humanity to receive a new spirit, a new kind of life: "It is no longer I who live, but it is Christ who lives in me" (Galatians 2:20).

When Jesus says, "I give you a new commandment: love one another as I have loved you," the commandment itself is not what is new. In fact, many before him had preached about love, both within and outside Israel. What is new here is the person, and thus the words "as *I* have loved you."

The Impetus of the Spirit

In Jesus there is a new way of transmitting the Spirit of the Father to human creatures, establishing between them and God a new mediation: "I know my own [sheep] and my own know me, just as the Father knows me and I know the Father" (John 10:14–15).

The Spirit, which emanates from the depths of every believer, makes greater demands than any codified law. What is more important is that the Spirit does not emanate from the outside, but from within.

Spirit and Law

Still, the commandment retains its value, and its function can be compared to that of an alarm bell. But a far vaster arena of obedience opens up in listening to the voice of the Spirit. One might give the example of the Easter duty to receive communion. On the one hand, the lukewarm believer is careful not to miss the days prescribed by ecclesiastical law, which he or she experiences as a kind of burden. On the other hand, the faithful believer, who feels a deeper need for union, will go to communion often and will not even recall the existence of the rule. Obedience to the voice of the Spirit is still obedience to a law, but it is obedience to an interior law that includes the requirements of the eternal law and makes them one with the person.

Chapter 32

The Covenant of Mount Sinai

God's Gift and Humankind's Response

As we know, the gift of God awaits a response from humankind. The Torah is offered by God to Israel; it is not imposed. The Lord offers a deeper knowledge of Himself to Israel; he does not oblige Israel to accept it: "*If* you obey my voice and keep my covenant, you shall be my treasured possession out of all the peoples" (Exodus 19:5). On its part, Israel freely pledges to do whatever the gift requires: "All that the Lord has spoken we will do, and we will be obedient" (Exodus 24:7). If we can say that Abraham responded to God's gift by believing, now humankind's response to the new gift of God is a renewed listening, manifested in obedience. The One God has made his will known, and humankind promises to follow it.

A New Relationship between God and Humankind

God's gift is met by Israel's desire to accept it; thus, a new bond, a new relationship, is established between God and his people. The terms of this new relationship are specified in Exodus 19:5ff.: "If you obey my voice . . . you shall be for me a priestly kingdom and a holy nation." Israel is solemnly invested with a priestly function in the midst of all peoples. It finds itself in a unique position before others who are not God's "particular possession," chosen and pledged to him. Yet, just as the priest does not keep God for himself but puts others in communication with him, so Israel must transmit the gift it has received to all humanity.

Formalized in Ritual

The new relationship with God must be given concrete form in a covenant ritual (described in Exodus 24:1ff.). The ritual does not ratify something that has already happened, but is an integral part of the covenant.
It is celebrated in a solemn way, using the blood of the sacrificed oxen.
Half of their blood is poured over the altar as an offering to God, while
the other half is scattered on the people. The blood ratifies the pact unit-
ing Israel to God, the blood which is *life* (Leviticus 17:11). It is life that
unites God and the people; only life could make it possible for the Lord
and Israel to become one "family," in a certain sense. The sharing of
blood constitutes the family, and the sharing of life makes Israel the people of God.

The union between God and the people is also revealed in the communion sacrifice that follows the blood ritual: "They beheld God, they
ate and drank" (Exodus 24:11). In the communion sacrifices in Israel, a
portion of the slain animal was burnt on the altar to signify the participation of the deity. What remained was eaten by those making the offering
during a meal in which the deity was considered to be the guest of honor.
The communal sharing of the meal expressed shared life.

Manifested in the Sign of the Covenant

Throughout time, a sign marks those who are members of the Sinai covenant with the Lord: the observance of the sabbath (Exodus 31:12ff.). As
compared to circumcision, the sign borne in the flesh of male Jews, the
sign of the Sinai covenant has a spiritual character. It is a setting aside of
a portion of time to God, as if it were a "tithe" of one's time. Initially, the
sabbath commandment obliged only rest, but as time passed, the celebration of particular rituals was added to it.

The Sinai covenant is an extremely important event in the history
of salvation; nevertheless, it is incomplete in some way. It points toward
a relationship with God that will become even more intimate and more
alive, as the prophet Jeremiah indicates: "The days are surely coming,
says the Lord, when I will make a new covenant with the house of Israel
and the house of Judah. . . . This is the covenant that I will make with
the house of Israel after those days, says the Lord: I will put my law

within them, and I will write it on their hearts and I will be their God and they shall be my people" (Jeremiah 31:31–33). Another stage in this waiting is the "new and everlasting covenant," which Jesus inaugurated and in which we now live, carried forward to that day when "God will be all in all."

Chapter 33

The Sanctuary

God's Presence in Israel

The new relationship between the Lord and Israel that is established in the covenant is given concrete form in the particular presence of God in the midst of His people. Initially, God's presence is both hidden and revealed by the cloud that guides Israel in the desert (Exodus 13:21; 24:15; Numbers 12:5ff.). The cloud hides God's presence from human eyes, which could not bear the divine brightness and splendor. At the same time, the cloud is the sign, the material object that indicates God's presence.

The Signs of God's Presence

After the gift of the Torah, the sanctuary was built in accordance with the Lord's instructions to Moses, as described in Exodus 25:9ff. It somehow reproduced the celestial dwelling of God. The sanctuary, initially carried with the people in their wandering, was made permanent through Solomon's work. After David's conquest of Jerusalem, his son Solomon built the Temple of Jerusalem. The Ark was placed in the innermost and holiest part of the Temple, the Holy of Holies. Destroyed by the Babylonians in 586 BCE, it was reconstructed on a more modest scale by the Jews on their return from exile. Herod the Great restored it to great magnificence around the time of the birth of Jesus. This "Second Temple" was destroyed by the Romans in 70 CE, never to be rebuilt—resulting in the emergence of the synagogue.

The Temple owed its particular sanctity to the presence of the Tablets of the Law, encased in the Ark and placed in the innermost and holiest part of the Temple.

Although the immensity of God is in no way limited—"even heaven and the highest heaven cannot contain you" (1 Kings 8:27)—the Temple is the focus of God's presence among the people. The term often used in Hebrew—"the tent of meeting," the sanctuary of the nomadic period—defines the Temple as the place where the people meet their God. A mysterious relationship binds the Temple with heaven. It is the place about which the Lord said, "Here will be my name"; thus, Solomon can ask with confidence, "Hear the plea of your servant and of your people Israel when they pray toward this place; O hear in heaven your dwelling place; heed and forgive" (1 Kings 8:30).

The "Temple of His Body"

In the New Testament, according to the gospel of John, Jesus identifies himself with the Temple: "Destroy this temple, and in three days I will raise it up." John goes on to explain: "But he was speaking of the temple of his body" (John 2:19ff.). The presence of God is given form in a living *Person*. In the New Testament everything is dynamic and, one could say, "existential." The "place" of God's presence is the very person of Christ. The believers themselves are "living stones" of the "spiritual temple" (1 Peter 2:4–5).

Examination of this reality again reveals the "golden thread" that connects history throughout its various phases. This history projects us toward a time when all that is created will be transformed and become a place of worship, when "every creature in heaven and on earth and under the earth and in the sea, and all that is in them" shall sing praises and honor to God and to his Christ (Revelation 5:13).

Chapter 34

The Typology of the Story of Moses

The great adventure that Israel lives at the time of its deliverance from Egypt does not exist within a vacuum. When considered alone, the Exodus is full of richness; yet it directs us toward the future and the completion of what has been foreshadowed and prepared. As a result, one must view this event in light of the redemption realized in Christ and its further development in the Church as she awaits the Parousia.

The typology of the story of Moses is primarily the typology of the Exodus. The Church is abundantly nourished by it, particularly during the Easter season. In Christ's death and resurrection the Church lives an experience of faith similar to Israel's experience of the Exodus. In fleeing Egypt, Israel renounces a life of subjugation, but also gives up a life of certain comforts. Upon reaching the opposite shore of the Red Sea, Israel has escaped death and is born as the free people of God. Similarly, Jesus renounces life and accepts death, thus giving birth to a new branch of God's people: the Church. The death and resurrection of Christ is for the Church what the Exodus is for Israel.

Christological Typology

The christological typology is delineated in two comparisons: Jesus and Moses, and Jesus and the paschal lamb.

Jesus and Moses

Inasmuch as Moses is liberator of the people, a teacher and the mediator of the gift of the Torah, his mission is tied to that of Jesus. In presenting

Jesus as the lawgiver who synthesizes his "Torah" in his discourse "on the mountain," the author of Matthew establishes a relationship between Jesus and Moses, who had received the Torah on Mount Sinai (Matthew 5:1ff.). Later, Cyril of Jerusalem notes,

> God sent Moses to deliver the Jews. . . . Let us pass from the old things to the new, from the type to the reality. There we have Moses sent by God to Egypt, here we have the Christ sent by the Father into the world; there we deal with the matter of freeing an oppressed people from Egypt, here we deal with the matter of rescuing humankind from the tyranny of the world of sin. There the blood of the lamb sends the angel of death away, here the blood of the True Lamb, Jesus Christ, causes evil to flee; there the tyrant pursues the people as far as the sea, here the impudent and bold devil pursues them as far as the sacred fount; one is drowned in the sea, the other is annihilated in the healing water.[28]

Jesus and the Paschal Lamb

More frequent is the comparison between Jesus and the paschal lamb, which saves from death. This comparison is present already in John 19:36. Furthermore, according to the chronology of John's gospel, Jesus died at the hour when the paschal lamb was being sacrificed in the Temple, the memorial of the lamb that saved the Jews from the angel of death in the Exodus; this was the hour when Jesus' mission was accomplished.

In his first letter to the Corinthians, Saint Paul explicitly states, "Our paschal lamb, Christ, has been sacrificed" (1 Corinthians 5:7). This statement is repeated in the Easter preface.

In Peter's first letter, perhaps addressed to neophytes and therefore also reflecting an Easter setting, the listeners are reminded of their ransom by Jesus, not with silver or gold or any such corruptible thing "but with the precious blood of Christ, like that of a lamb without defect or blemish. He was destined before the foundation of the world, but was revealed at the end of the ages for your sake. Through him you have come to trust in God, who raised him from the dead" (1 Peter 1:19ff.).

The book of Revelation points to the time when the triumphant Christ will be as a "lamb standing as if it had been slaughtered" (5:6; cf. 14:1).

Among the Fathers of the Church, Aphraetes develops the parallel between the Jewish Passover and the Christian Easter with the words

> At Passover, the Jews fled from Pharaoh's bondage; on the days of the cruci-fixion we are set free from Satan's captivity. The Jews sacrificed a lamb and were rescued from the angel of death by its blood; we are delivered from the works of corruption we have done by the blood of the Beloved Son. They had Moses as a guide; we have Jesus as our leader and Savior. Moses parted the waters of the sea for them to cross over it; our Savior opened and broke the doors of hell and, when he descended into its depths, he opened the way and showed that way to all those who ought to believe in him.[29]

The paschal liturgy carries on this tradition. On Holy Thursday the precepts regarding the sacrifice of the lamb are read from Exodus 12:1ff. The lamb that saved the Jews from death, making it possible for them to become the free people of God, is the type of the Lamb who will give eternal life to humankind with his death.

The invocations addressed to the "Lamb of God" during the Mass are also noteworthy in this regard.

Sacramental Typology

The events of the Exodus signify for the Jews a religious experience sim-ilar to the Christian experience of the sacraments, although on different levels. In the Exodus the Jews meet a God who rescues and sustains them; Christians are delivered from the domination of Satan in baptism, and receive the food of eternal life in the Eucharist. In fact, sacramental typology is essentially baptismal and Eucharistic.

Baptism and the Exodus: The Waters of Deliverance

The comparison between the liberating waters of the Red Sea and the liberating waters of baptism is a classical element in the instruction of catechumens. Tertullian says:

> The people freed from Egypt, in crossing the water, escape from the power of the Egyptian king; the water annihilates the king himself and all his troops. What analogy is clearer than that of the sacrament of baptism? The pagans are delivered from the world, and this is done by means of the water; they abandon the devil, their old tyrant, who is engulfed by the water.[30]

Furthermore, Saint Ambrose speaks of the saving waters and considers how baptism is prefigured in the Jews' crossing of the sea "when the Egyptian perishes while the Jew is saved. What other teaching do we receive but that guilt is engulfed and error abolished, while piety and innocence remain intact?"[31]

In the liturgy of the Easter Vigil, the third reading is taken from Exodus 14:15—15:1, which narrates the miraculous crossing of the sea and is interpreted in the prayer which follows the reading: "[Y]ou once bestowed on a single people, freeing them from Pharaoh's persecution by the power of your right hand, now you bring about as the salvation of the nations through the waters of rebirth. . . ."

Also, Moses' changing of the waters of Marah from bitter to sweet (Exodus 15:23ff.) is a symbol of baptism. In this regard Tertullian says,

> Another symbol is that of the water which was made drinkable and sweet by Moses' throwing a piece of wood into it. That wood was Christ who himself cures the waters which were once poisoned and bitter. He changes them into healing, refreshing waters, the waters of baptism.[32]

The same miracle is recalled during the consecration of the baptismal waters during the Easter Vigil. Among the pictorial representations in the oldest catacombs (those of Saints Domitilla and Priscilla), the figure of Moses causing the water to spring from the rock is often depicted and is usually interpreted as a baptismal symbol. Saint Cyprian speaks of Christ who is "the rock" and who "was struck" by the lance during his crucifixion.

Eucharist and Manna: The Food of Life

Already in Psalm 105:40, manna is called "bread of heaven." Eucharistic typology goes back to Jesus himself. When reminded by the crowd about the miraculous manna in the wilderness, Jesus replies, "I am the bread of life" (John 6:30ff.).

Theodotus offers an example of Eucharistic typology:

> Manna represents divine nourishment; the water from the rock represents the blood of the Savior. Indeed, just as the Jews, after crossing the Red Sea, tasted a marvelous nourishment that came from an extraordinary source, we, too, after the healing immersion, participate in the divine mysteries.[33]

During the adoration of the cross on Good Friday, the "Reproaches," which are often replaced by other texts so that they might not be interpreted to be anti-Semitic, include the words, "I fed you with manna in the desert, and on me you rained blows and lashes."

Saint Basil's writings synthesize many typological elements of the Exodus:

> The image is in fact a manifestation of things that are awaited, by means of an imitation, which gives a preview of future events, so that we will be able to recognize them when they occur. Thus, the rock is the type of Christ, and the water is the image of the enlivening power of the word. Manna is the figure of living bread "that comes down from heaven"; the serpent placed on the staff is the image of the healing passion which is consumed on the cross. In the same way, the Exodus is narrated as a clue to those who will be saved by means of baptism. . . . The wise person can comprehend these things: how the sea can be the type of baptism because it separates the people from the pharaoh, how this baptismal bath separates us from the devil. The enemy was killed by the sea itself; in the same way our hostility toward God is killed in baptism. The people emerge from the sea safe and sound and saved; we rise again from the waters as the living among the dead, saved by the grace of the One who has called us.[34]

Chapter 35

The Exodus and Parousia

The Exodus and Eschatological Deliverance

"On that day" when God's plan will be fully realized the full realization will bear some likenesses to the Exodus, where it had a beginning.

Just as the Exodus is liberation *par excellence* for Israel, so the Parousia will be liberation on the cosmic level. Recall what was said in this regard about creation and the flood. The heavens and the earth will be renewed because the whole of creation will be delivered from its subjugation to Satan (Romans 8:18ff.). The deliverance that will occur "on that day" will not be witnessed by only a few but will happen before the eyes of all people, and even the ends of the earth will see it. Also "on that day," "the Lord will go before you, and the God of Israel will be your rear guard" (Isaiah 52:12).

A marvelous new pathway will be opened up in the wilderness and on it the redeemed will travel (Isaiah 43:16–21). Yet "on that day," it will no longer be only Israel who treads that highway, but all peoples (Isaiah 11:11–16; cf. Isaiah 40:3–5). The "pathway" has already been opened up; what is awaited is that all peoples walk on it together.

Now the words of the prophet can be interpreted in light of the words of Christ, who says: "I am the Way" (John 14:6). Christ is the way that leads to the Father and to his kingdom.

As already noted, the Church reads the narrative of the Exodus (Exodus 14:15—15:1) during the Easter Vigil and prays immediately afterward that "the whole world may become children of Abraham and inherit the dignity of Israel's birthright."

During the Passover liturgy, the synagogue commemorates the deliverance from Egypt and concludes the celebration, praying that "the prophet Elijah and the Messiah, the son of your servant David, may come soon in our day and bring us the good news."

Both the synagogue and the Church project Israel's deliverance from Egypt toward the final deliverance in the end times.

Chapter 36

Bible-Liturgy: A Unity

In light of all that has been said, it becomes clear that the Bible and the liturgy—I would prefer to say Bible-liturgy—form a unity. There are not two separate entities: a Bible that is read and studied and Liturgy that is a lived experience. Rather, there is the Bible that is lived in the Liturgy.

Knowledge of the Old Testament makes all that we live in the Liturgy more evident to us—I would say more tangible—because it enables us to see certain supernatural realities reflected in the concreteness of human events. All that might be simply incomprehensible or lost to us just because it is supernatural becomes obvious and concrete when contemplated through the facts and events brought to our attention in the Liturgy.

Furthermore, in our sacramental life we live events of great importance in concentrated form. We see that these events have been realized gradually, through thousands of years of development, and this realization makes it easier to comprehend the underlying purpose in the event. More importantly, it makes our way of living these events fuller.

Thus, the Bible is essential for our liturgical life. Furthermore, in light of the unity of the Bible and the Liturgy, the Liturgy is the *only* place where the Bible can be fully comprehended. And when I say "Liturgy" here, I am not referring to the part of the Liturgy that is specifically dedicated to the Word, but rather to the heart of Liturgy: the Eucharist.

Chapter 37

The Prophets

ESSENTIAL TEXTS TO READ: (Note: Given the vastness of prophetic literature, it is difficult to choose particular texts to read): Isaiah 1:1–20; 6:1–13; 10:33—11:16; 35:1–10; 40:1–31; 60:1–22; Jeremiah 31:31–34, 36–38; Ezekiel 34:1–31. The "Songs of the Suffering Servant" will be referred to in Chapter 39 of this book.

The Prophet as One Who Listens to God's Word

The prophet holds the same position in Israel that the philosopher holds in Greece or the hero holds in other civilizations. In Israel the prophet personifies the spirit of the people better than anyone else.

On what basis is one identified as a prophet? The prophet is characterized by a particular capacity to listen to God. If the prophet can be identified as a *voice*—the voice of God in the midst of people—it is because he has first been an *ear,* straining to listen to what God has made known to him. The prophet is the spokesman of the Jewish people because in him is found the highest level of the fundamental religious attitude of Israel, proclaimed in the words, *"Hear,* O Israel, the Lord is our God, the Lord alone" (Deuteronomy 6:4ff.).

The spirituality of Israel can be defined as a spirituality of listening; thus, where there is Jewish spirituality, there is prophecy. At the dawn of the history of Israel there is already a prophet, Abraham (Genesis 20:7), and Moses is said to be the greatest prophet in Israel. Nathan played the role of harsh judge in relation to David (2 Samuel 11ff.), when he read in David's heart the crime David had committed with Bathsheba and conveyed to him the word of the Lord on the matter. The miracles and works of Elijah and Elisha in Jewish history fill the chronicles of Israel (ninth century BCE).

However, there is a period referred to specifically as the "period of the prophets." It begins in the eighth century BCE and concludes around the third century BCE. This is the period of the so-called "literary prophets," who are known because their preaching is preserved in the books of the Bible bearing their names: the four major prophets (Isaiah, Jeremiah, Ezekiel, and Daniel), and the twelve minor prophets, so named because they left smaller amounts of writing.

While scripture records many of the deeds and little of the preaching of the earlier prophets (such as Abraham and Moses), little is known about the lives of the "literary prophets," although much of their preaching has been preserved. Because of this, some scholars maintain that Israel's prophetic tradition was initially one of "wonderworkers," and only later became a prophetic tradition in the true sense of the word. However, this is a false distinction, since the telltale mark of the prophet is a particular listening stance before God that allows the prophet to be God's mouthpiece. Nevertheless, the historical books that tell us about the previous generation of prophets focus primarily on what they accomplished, while the prophetic books that preserve the memory of the literary prophets are chiefly concerned with their teachings. While the biblical prophet is always the voice of God among people, different scriptural genres highlight different aspects of prophetic ministry.

The Prophet as Interpreter of History

The literary prophets emerge in a specific period of the history of salvation and have their own particular task: to interpret history. Israel had already lived fundamental moments of its sacred history, meeting God in its journey and living its history together with and guided by God. The prophet now comes to interpret the events experienced by Israel and to reveal their hidden meaning. The prophet says he has participated in the "counsel of God" (Amos 3:7). Thus, he has been allowed to penetrate the *mysterium* of history and so shares in God's secret intentions.

It is interesting to note that the great prophets appear in the history of Israel when the monarchy begins a slow decline (eighth century BCE).

When the darkness has begun to spread over the people, the task of the prophet is to point to the constant presence—in the darkness and in spite of it—of the light of God, and to the inexhaustible faithfulness of the love of God: "I have loved you with an everlasting love" (Jeremiah 31:3).

The Meaning of the Word "Prophet"

In sharing his secrets, the Lord of Israel establishes a particular relationship with the prophets; the Lord enriches them with a gift that leads to a mission. The prophet lends his ear—and, even more, his heart—to the word of God, not to keep it for himself but to share it with all people, so they might take instruction from it. The word "prophet" comes from Greek and means "one who speaks for another"; the word is used to translate the Hebrew term *nabi.* A grammatical examination of this word makes clear the position of the prophet before God and before the people.

Grammatically, the word prophet *(nabi)* is an "action noun" that is expressed in the passive form. Examination of the word's form thus indicates passivity and activity within the one being identified by the term. The prophet allows an action to be done to him in order to perform another action in response. The prophet is passive before God in receiving God's message, allowing it to penetrate and nourish him. Once the word of God has penetrated the prophet, it leads to action. This action is not initiated by the human being; rather, it originates in God. On this issue, Jeremiah speaks in terms of seduction: "O Lord, you have enticed me, and I was enticed" (Jeremiah 20:7).

Power enters the prophet, a power that is not his own. This power comes from outside the prophet, but it becomes one with him. Ezekiel clarifies this point when he speaks of having eaten the scroll that contained the word of God; he "ate it; and in [his] mouth it was as sweet as honey" (Ezekiel 3:2). He is nourished by it, and thus the word of God becomes his blood and his life.

Often, at the initiation of their vocation, the prophets receive a contact similar to the one reported by Ezekiel. Jeremiah tells how the Lord touched his mouth and said to him, "Now I have put my words in your mouth" (Jeremiah 1:9). In this instance scripture presents the prophet at the very moment when he experiences the action done to him by the Lord. In other cases the account is less explicit, but it is always the action of the Lord that transforms the prophet and makes him a "new man." Amos was a herdsman and a cultivator of sycamores, but the Lord "snatched" him, taking him from his herds and telling him, "Go, prophesy to my people Israel" (Amos 7:15).

Chapter 38

The Struggle of the Prophet

The Struggle with God

In the Old Testament the first struggle the prophet has is with God himself, who calls the prophet to ministry. The prophet is very aware of the heavy burden such ministry involves, and he attempts to flee from it. He is, after all, responding in the same way that so many others did in the face of God's call. Moses balked at it (Exodus 3); Jeremiah uses the excuse that he is much too young. The only exception to this apparent norm is the response of Isaiah (Isaiah 6:1–8).

In the book of Jonah, this attitude is carried to extremes. The Lord calls Jonah to go and preach to the people of Nineveh. Having received the call, Jonah goes down to the sea, not to depart for Nineveh, but for Tarshish (perhaps Tartessos in Spain, the farthest known western land). Today, some understand the book of Jonah as a sample of a literary genre whose aim is similar to that of the parable; thus its opening typifies the prophet's first encounter with the call of God, in which one's first reaction is flight.

Such resistance is admittedly reasonable, for the prophet knows he will have to absorb and repeat the word of the Lord. He also knows that God's word is "a fire" (Jeremiah 5:14), and "like a hammer [that] breaks a rock" (Jeremiah 23:29). The prophet knows that the first rock this particular hammer will shatter is his own heart, which would prefer to ignore the wicked ways of human beings and the evils that threaten the people.

The Struggle with the People

The prophet knows that the fire of God's word purifies, but that, in purifying, it burns. Although there are those who accept the suffering that the purification brings, there are others who, in order not to feel the burning of the word of the Lord, try to extinguish the flame. When the wicked person is unable to silence the word itself, he tries to silence the mouth that repeats the word. After all, the prophet knows that his mission will sometimes expose him to violent persecutions by the people and the rulers (Jeremiah 26:1ff.; 36:1ff.). In any case, the prophet will be met with incomprehension on the part of the people who try to ignore his words, and with derision on the part of those who believe him to be mad or possessed. The prophet will find himself condemned always to solitude, and to swimming against the current.

It is not surprising, then, that even the greatest prophets (Moses, Elijah) had moments of weakness, moments when they preferred death to the great burden of the prophetic ministry. Jeremiah, for whom the word of the Lord became "a cause for insult and derision," says, "I will not speak in his name anymore." But God's word, which is "a fire burning," grows into a fiery blaze in his bones, and he cannot contain it within himself (Jeremiah 20:7ff.). Thus, the prophet soon continues his mission with the attitude of one who has been seduced, and therefore acts against his own will in a sense.

The False Prophets

To make the task of the prophet even more difficult, there are also those prophets whom no one has called, and who "follow their own spirit" (Ezekiel 13:1ff.). These prophets do not repeat the word of the Lord, but "their own private delusions." They continue to announce peace "when there is no peace." The choice between the fiery words of a true prophet and the pleasing words of a false prophet might appear to be an easy one, yet between the preaching of the two, there is the same difference which separates the straw from the wheat (Jeremiah 23:25ff.). The false prophets sometimes place themselves in direct conflict with the prophets of God, and some of the dramatic clashes between them are recorded in the Bible (Jeremiah 28:1ff.).

In spite of all the difficulties the prophet might encounter in himself and in others, he remains faithful to his mission with his whole being. Indeed, the mission of the prophet involves the whole life of the one called by the Lord. When the prophet is nourished by the word of God, as Ezekiel was, there is no longer anything in him which is not permeated by it; the very *life* of the prophet becomes *prophecy*. In contrast to the predictions that sorcerers and fortune-tellers give, Isaiah (8:16ff.) offers himself and his children as "signs and portents in Israel from the Lord of hosts." Here, we are already on the track that leads to Jesus, who will preach through his Person rather than his words—with his suffering, death, and resurrection. To those who ask for a sign, Jesus will answer that the sign he will give them will be "that of Jonah," the act by which all his earthly life is epitomized.

Chapter 39

The Preaching of
the Prophets

The prophetic literature is a literary genre unto itself in the Bible; it has particular characteristics as to its content and the manner in which it has been collected and compiled. The teaching of the prophet is chiefly a spoken one. However, sometimes the Lord himself commands the prophet to write. At times the prophet himself records his teaching; at other times he is assisted by a secretary to whom he dictates the message word for word (Jeremiah 36:1ff.).

Furthermore, although the prophet may have been a loner of sorts, he often had a circle of disciples who would have listened intensely to the words he spoke, memorized them according to the custom of the times, and transmitted them to others, either orally or in written form. This explains the fragmentary character of much prophetic literature.

Given the breadth and variety of prophetic preaching, it is difficult to offer a guide to it in a few words. Basically, prophetic preaching has two principal thrusts: messianic and moral. In the end, however, this apparent division can be reconfigured as a unity, because the entire prophetic mission is aimed at the preparation for the coming of the Kingdom of God and for the one who will bring its inauguration, the Messiah. It is possible to synthesize prophetic preaching by saying that it deals with only one theme: salvation. The prophets speak of the Person who will bring salvation (messianic preaching), and of the way of preparing one's heart for that Person's coming (moral preaching).

Messianic Preaching

The term "messianism" is derived from "Messiah" and is a synonym of "Christianity," derived from "Christ." "Messiah" and "Christ" are synonyms; the first comes from Hebrew and the second from Greek. Both terms point to the Messiah as the one who has received anointing, the means of participating in the sacred power of God. The source of power and of life is God. The Messiah, who stands in particular relationship to God, is, by definition, the anointed one.

Messianism Is Waiting

Messianism can be defined as waiting, a waiting which is tied to a particular conception of time. Time can be understood in various ways. One conception of time, prevalent in certain periods in the Greek world, sees it as cyclical in nature, always returning to itself, wearing out and being consumed. In this view, the best remains in the past, gone for good, without hope of return. Another similar concept sees birth as the beginning of a process of degeneration, a process which cannot be stopped.

Still another concept of time views it as unfolding in a straight line. According to this concept, every moment that passes brings something new. Far from bringing impoverishment, the passage of time brings enrichment and progress. Moreover, the best is yet to come; today is better than yesterday, and tomorrow will be better than today. If the cyclical conception of time is pessimistic and leads to unproductive nostalgia, the conception of time as unfolding in a straight line is essentially dynamic and prolific in energy and rich in hope.

This linear understanding of time is prevalent in the Jewish world. In the Bible, everything waits expectantly for an era of well-being, of fertility, of an abundance of God's spirit. In many texts, the arrival of this era is connected to the arrival of a Person who will be the Messiah; in other texts it comes directly from God. This is called messianism without a Messiah.

When did this waiting begin in Israel? It is intrinsic to the mind of Israel, an integral part of its understanding of life, as old as Israel itself. Abraham, the first patriarch, based his life on a promise, waiting for its fulfillment. Nevertheless, the messianic waiting seems to have been concretized primarily with the institution of the monarchy, and we can explain why.

Waiting for an Ideal King

According to the Jews, royalty is the divine attribute of excellence: God renders justice to his people and defends the rights of the weak, the orphan and the widow. God guides the wars of Israel, intervening with celestial armies. God governs, providing for the needs of his people. The abilities to render justice, to direct wars, and to govern are essentially royal attributes. With the institution of the monarchy, God "lends" some of these attributes to the king in order to qualify him for his duties; this transaction occurs through the king's anointing. In this way the king enters into union with the divine power found in God. Nevertheless, an abyss will always separate the omnipotent royalty of God from the royalty of the human king. The messianic idea rises out of this disparity between the Jews' royal ideal—in which only the Lord is king—and the reality represented by a human king. It stems precisely from the inability of the Jews to allow their royal ideal to be confined to a human institution. Even if no king of Israel satisfied their ideal, nevertheless, the king, the "anointed one" of their longing, would still come at a future time. The true messianic ideal could not be satisfied other than in a king who would be a God-king.

For Israel the coming of the Messiah will be reflected in nature; there will then be "new heavens and a new earth." There will be a particular abundance of the produce of the earth, and nature will know a new and eternal spring; therefore, "he who sows will be met by he who reaps." Peace will reign among the animals and between people and animals, because humankind will reestablish its authority over the subhuman world (Isaiah 11:6ff.). Every disability in human beings will disappear: There will no longer be anyone who is deaf or blind or lame (Isaiah 29:18ff.; 35:1ff.).

All of this will come to pass because the earth will overflow with the abundance of the spirit of God, and those gifts that have been bestowed on a few throughout time will then be showered on all (Joel 3:1ff.).

Waiting for an Abundance of Spirit

There will be an abundance of the spirit of God, because the Messiah who comes will himself be filled with spirit of God (Isaiah 10:33—11:1ff.), and he will be empowered to shower it on others. His coming will be preceded by a period of upheaval and havoc, which the prophet compares to the hewing down of a forest of large trees; but in the midst of the uproar, a shoot will spring forth. After such a great commotion a shoot would seem to be an insignificant detail, but upon that shoot will alight the spirit of the Lord. With its mysterious energy, it will become like a signal to the peoples (Isaiah 11:10), and all the people will turn toward it.

The prophets use various images in introducing the Messiah: He is a powerful king (Psalm 72:8ff.); he is a just judge (Isaiah 11:3ff.); he is the defender of the lowly and the weak, and the comforter of the brokenhearted (Isaiah 61:1ff.). Here, we will focus on two particular images: the Messiah as light and the Messiah as redeemer.

The Messiah as Bearer of Light

The image of the Messiah as *light* is among the most frequent (Isaiah 8:23—9:1ff., and so on) and is used by Jesus, who says of himself: "I am the light of the world." He demonstrates this by giving sight and faith to the man born blind (John 9:7ff.). The prophets frequently use images (light, water, and so on); in these instances they are being poets in the true sense of the word. The term "poetic" is often used as a synonym for the fantastic or imaginary. However, the word "poet" comes from the Greek *poiein,* meaning "to make," and points to the poet as one who "makes" images that accurately represent reality. The poet expresses concrete reality through images, and these images adhere strictly to the realities they express. Accordingly, when the prophet says that the Messiah is light or that he will bring light to the world, it is not just a beautiful image of the poet's choosing; rather, it is the true reality.

We, too, are accustomed to expressing knowledge with terms that refer to light. We say that an idea is "clear to me," "I am enlightened, I understand," and so on. Thus, the prophet can say that the Messiah will bring light into the world because he will bring people a deeper and more intimate knowledge of God. Only Jesus reveals that the one God is also the triune God. Furthermore, while outside Israel God is known primarily through the contemplation of nature, within Israel God is known particularly through his works in history, and from redemption onward, the Father is known through the Son.

The Messiah as Redeemer

One other messianic concept remains to be examined. This concept, found only in a few fragments of the book of Isaiah, does not reappear in the prophetic tradition of Israel. It deals with the concept of the Messiah as the one who, although innocent, suffers in order to expiate the sins of others.

The Problem of the Suffering of the Just

The concept of a suffering Messiah is framed by the problem of the suffering of the just, a problem that surfaces many other times in the Old Testament, particularly in the prophets and in the Psalms, which echo prophetic preaching. The prophets' faith in God is firm, but they cannot avoid asking themselves why "the wicked" seem to prosper, while the just are in distress. Jeremiah wishes to debate with the Lord on this point (Jeremiah 12:1ff.).

Originally, the problem was resolved in the Hebrew scriptures by affirming that the one who suffers deserves the suffering in some way because of sin. This was still the prevailing mentality in the time of Jesus. When the apostles encountered the man born blind, they asked the Teacher who had sinned—the blind man, or his parents—for him to deserve such misfortune. Obviously the reality of suffering often refutes such a principle. But why, then, do the just suffer?

The Book of Job

The book of Job seeks to deal with this very question. The protagonist Job is presented as a type of a perfectly just person, and yet he suffers serious misfortune. The friends around him repeat the common adage: he who suffers has certainly sinned. Job's repeated assertions of his innocence are not successful in silencing them. God himself brings an end to the discussion. The Lord places before Job several proofs of his immense power.

> Where were you when I laid the foundation of the earth, when I marked the bounds of the sea, saying to it: "Come thus far and no farther?" Have you instructed the heavenly bodies as to their pathways? Do you know the place where the rain and hail are kept?" (Job 38, paraphrased)

When confronted with these questions, Job can only remain silent and acknowledge his smallness before the infinite greatness of God. How can one ask for an explanation of the work of a God so great? In the face of so much power, one cannot but surrender and bow one's head.

But the problem is not solved. God has closed Job's mouth, but God has not explained what the suffering just one has asked: "Why do I suffer? These are my works, and these are my sufferings; but where is your justice?" This question is not answered in the book of Job. To obtain an answer, one must read the songs of the suffering servant.[35]

The Songs of the Suffering Servant

Isaiah 42:1–7. This passage introduces the "Servant of God" as one who has been endowed with the spirit of God and is a person of particular sensitivity. His task is to bring justice to the ends of the earth, extending to all the covenant of the Lord with his people.

Isaiah 49:1–6. The Servant himself speaks, alluding to the failure of his mission, a failure that nevertheless did not weaken his faith in God. Once again, the universality of his mission is confirmed.

Isaiah 50:1–6. The Servant has received knowledge from the Lord which is not given to other people (verse 5). He has suffered and has not resisted the suffering; rather, he has continued to put his faith in the Lord all the more.

Isaiah 52:13—53:12. The description of the sufferings of the Servant is completed here, and an explanation is given: He is struck down for the people's sins; to him falls the punishment that saves all people; his suffering is the expiation, not for his sins—because the servant is without sin—but for the sins of others.

At this point, the problem of suffering leaves the realm of the individual, and the solution is no longer sought in the moral state of the individual who suffers. While the suffering of Job remains a question, the suffering of the Servant of the Lord is justified and explained: Though the one being afflicted is innocent, "he has taken our sins upon himself."

The Suffering Is Atonement for the Evil of the World

The sufferings of the innocent no longer succeed in casting a shadow on the justice of God. The guilty one expiates his own sin with his own contrition; the innocent one expiates the sin of others by his own sorrows.

The Christian tradition has always seen in Jesus the prophetic figure of the suffering servant who expiates the sin of the world. Already in the gospel of Mark (1:11), Jesus' willingness to receive the baptism of repentance, even though he is without sin, offers an allusion to the servant whom the Lord has chosen and on whom the spirit of God rests.

In our current lectionary, the servant songs are read during Holy Week.

In the Jewish tradition, the figure of the servant in Isaiah sometimes refers to an individual and sometimes to Israel itself, the people who suffered the exile. This interpretation gradually prevailed after the tragic events of 135 CE: the destruction of Jerusalem by Hadrian, the changing of the name of the city to Aelia Capitolina and of the country to Palestine, and the erection of pagan temples on ancient places of worship. This interpretation has acquired particular significance today, in light of the Holocaust.

The texts have multiple meanings and multiple reverberations that echo through the centuries. The words illuminate the events, but the events also illuminate the words. Thus, as sacred history gradually unfolds, it becomes possible to recognize the allusions in the words of the prophets, which come to reveal ever broader horizons of meaning.

The Jewish interpretation does not exclude the Christian one. According to Remaud,[36] there is only one suffering servant who is at the same time both Jesus and Israel. Both have lived in full the destiny of the suffering just one, whom God alone recognizes and who carries the burden of the sin of the world. Both experienced the silence of God that seems to favor the adversaries; yet, neither of them ceased believing in

God, nor did they stop praying, even when it seemed God had abandoned them. Jesus' "My God, my God, why have you forsaken me?" and what the Jews refer to as God's "hiding his face" echo one another.

Moral Preaching

The subjects included in the prophets' moral preaching are many and varied. We will limit ourselves to one point, common to all the prophets and particularly frequent in their preaching. The moral preaching of the prophets is connected to that of the New Testament. The primary characteristic of New Testament morality is that it is tied to a relationship with a Person. Already in the Old Testament, God is a Person. The Jew does not believe in a divinity that is an impersonal power, an energy pervading creation. The God of the Jew is a being endowed with infinite knowledge and love, the source of all power, all energy, all life. Thus, it follows that in the Old Testament there are already moral exigencies that are similar to those characterizing Christian morality.

The Importance of the Intention of the Heart

One of the most important points that emerge from the particular character of Christian morality—synthesized in the formula "imitation of Christ"—is the need for a constant interior attitude. While a code of conduct can be satisfactorily adhered to, though perhaps only in a formal, superficial manner, a relationship with a Person calls for sincerity of heart beyond the act itself.

Already in the Old Testament, the prophets and the psalmists speak of God as the One "who scrutinizes the loins and the heart" (loins and heart in the Old Testament are the seat of knowledge and consciousness, of thought and feeling). God is the one who knows the "sitting down and the rising up," "the comings and the goings" of his faithful ones. Such expressions affirm that God knows every single action, every movement of the human heart. Therefore, the prophets already give priority to the *intention of the heart*. The sacrifice that pleases God is the one offered by a contrite heart (Psalm 51). The prayer recited while raising "hands covered with innocent blood" cannot be accepted. Sacrificial worship is devalued (Isaiah 1:1ff.) when it is not sustained and enlivened by the God's spirit. Animal sacrifices and fasting can be empty acts. Sabbath rest means not merely abstention from work, but an offering of one's very thoughts to God (Amos 8:6). The Lord is the God of life, and what the Lord desires is the commitment of one's whole life to him. The requirements of the God of Israel are all-embracing; they correspond to the fullness of the blessings which God showers on his faithful ones.

The words of the prophets foreshadow Jesus' admonition: "Not everyone who says to me, 'Lord, Lord,' will enter the kingdom of heaven, but only the one who does the will of my Father" (Matthew 7:21).

The teaching relating to the heart's intention *(kawwana)* in the performance of the works has also been developed in the post-biblical Jewish tradition, and has assumed a particular importance in the Jewish mystical tradition. In this vein, when addressing the delegates to the Episcopal Conference on Jewish-Christian Relations (March 6, 1982), Pope John Paul II spoke of the blossoming, more than 2000 years ago, of a "new branch on the one trunk" of the people of God.

Chapter 40

Between the Old and New Testaments[37]

We have already attempted to explain in some way what the coming of Jesus of Nazareth represents in the unfolding of the history of salvation, as well as the particularity and uniqueness of the divine intervention that is fulfilled through him.

We have also said how, in the infinite wealth of a new presence of God in the midst of humankind, a schism takes place in God's people. One branch recognizes Jesus as the Messiah, the Son of God, and accepts the messianic doctrine as an unfolding process already in progress. This process is mysterious, however, similar to the leaven fermenting in dough, waiting for the whole of creation to be enlivened by it. For the Jewish branch, Jesus is a great prophet and teacher in Israel, but the coming of the Messiah will be acknowledged only when its effects are evident.

Therefore, the Christian branch and the Jewish branch of God's people continue their journey in history along different pathways, enlivened by a common stretching towards the realization of the reign of God.

As a result of the destruction of Jerusalem and the Temple in 70 CE, Israel loses its political independence and is engulfed by the Roman Empire. Only in 1948, with the establishment of the State of Israel, is its political identity restored.

For almost 2,000 years most of the people of Israel have been scattered all over the world, while a small nucleus faithfully remained in the land of their ancestors. The Diaspora has allowed Israel to give witness to its religious values throughout the world and to contribute to the culture of humankind through its philosophers, physicians, musicians, scientists, and other gifted members.

In the following pages we will speak briefly of the first budding of the Christian branch of the people of God.

Chapter 41

Incarnation

We have spoken of the history of salvation as a gradual and progressive "incarnation" of God, an increasing manifestation of God through the perceivable. With the incarnation, history reaches a climax in which God makes himself visible through the sacred humanity of the Son.

Rooted in the Past, Yet Absolutely New

At the moment of the Incarnation, God's intention, God's *mysterion,* which had gradually been revealed to his servants the prophets, is now realized in the person of Jesus. Since its beginning, creation was waiting for the presence of the creature in whom God's image would be fully embodied; the unfolding history was waiting for God himself to be embodied in the person of Christ, restoring through him that order which Adam had spoiled.

The event of the Incarnation was always present in the mind of God and was therefore anticipated from the beginning of the world. Nevertheless, it comes as something entirely new. If the entire history of salvation is the history of God's intervention in the history of human beings, then never until the Incarnation did God intervene in such a direct way. If the whole history of salvation is the story of God's manifestation to people, never did God manifest himself so fully that whoever saw the human person of Christ could say, "You are the Christ, the Son of the living God."

The news of the Incarnation is so great that it is not easily grasped. With this in mind, it can be helpful to contemplate it in the light of other news that had preceded it, but that was in no way equal to it. Still, this work of comparison can aid our understanding.

The Incarnation in Relation to the Creation of Adam

Appearing at the end of the work of creation, Adam represents a totally new creature as compared to the creatures that preceded him. The Bible points this out in many ways.

At last there is a being whose eyes are open and capable of receiving images of God's creative work with an intelligent mind and a discerning heart, a being capable of recognizing God through these images and communicating with him. For the first time ever, a creature is given the task of cultivating and maintaining what God has created, of advancing the creative work of God, simultaneously imprinting creation with the mark of the creature made in God's image.

Everything is new in Adam; yet, everything will be "new" in a particular and incomparable way in the "new Adam." Sacred history, which opens with the creation of Adam and is charged with marvelous hopes, nearly collapses in the same moment it is begun because of humankind's failure to cooperate in the divine plan. However, the working of God's mercy immediately gives an inkling that history will resume its course and reach its goal, even if the journey will be laborious and the pathway altered.

A fundamental stage of this journey is the choice of Israel. It is another moment when everything "breathes the new."

The Incarnation and the Election of Israel

A tremor of expectation and hope begins to move through history when, among all the peoples in the world, God chooses one to be his "firstborn" (Exodus 4:22). All the peoples of the world can know God through the contemplation of the work of creation, but Israel has a particular relationship with God. Israel knows God through the contemplation of the events of its own life, and it lives these events in a particular union with God. Israel does not need to look outside itself to know God; instead, it knows God through a continuous dialogue with him. God, from whom Adam distanced himself in his rebellion, comes close to humankind anew and wants the history of this people to be God's own history in some way.

Thus, everything is new in Israel; but its newness is incomparable with fulfillment in Christ.

In Christ, for the first time, there appears a human being who places all of his humanity at the complete service of divinity. In him humanity is the docile and intelligent instrument of divinity in the highest possible manner. Of the many attempts of people throughout history to respond to the repeated and constant gift of God, the divine gift is finally met with the fullest and most worthy response possible from a human being.

The Perfect Human Response to God

The Son of Man is the greatest manifestation of the merciful and redeeming love of God; and, along with a downward movement from heaven to earth, "in the person of Jesus there is also a movement from earth to heaven, a movement from the human heart of the Son upwards to the Father."[38] There had never been a more perfect or timely movement in the history of humankind. At long last, a new bond between God and humankind is established and would remain forever, a bond in which God does not dwell in the *midst* of people, but "*in* the temple of his [Christ's] body" and, through him, *in* people.

Just as in Adam creation had a completely new creature, so in Christ history has a completely new human being.

Christ Brings New Life to the People

In fact, this extraordinary event is destined to be repeated and diffused, because the new Adam, who is like the first Adam but also different from him, is the founder, the firstborn of a kingdom of new people.

The Incarnation is a great event for its own sake, but also because of its effect on the whole of humanity. From that moment onward, the gift of new life and a different ontological relationship with God is offered through Christ. The person who is joined to Christ comes to share in the secrets of life within the Trinity through Christ's sacred humanity. A new life now flows through the spiritual veins of the human creature. This new life is God's life, transmitted through the humanity of the Risen Christ.

He Permeates the Entire Cosmos

The Incarnation is such a great event that it cannot be confined to the world of humankind alone but spreads out to enliven the whole cosmos. If the purpose of the Word becoming flesh was "that all of humankind might become divine through it," then to this we must add that

> the divinization of the human being, inasmuch as it affects his body, some- how affects the whole cosmos. For the entire cosmos serves as the theater and backdrop for the human creature in its bodily existence. The descent of the divine into the body of the human being implies and is, in some way, the transfiguration of the whole cosmos. . . . Christ's body is the firstfruit, not only of humankind but of all creation.[39]

If a new "blood" enlivens the spiritual veins of Christians, it is also true that a new surge of life now moves the cosmos in its innermost recesses, because divinity has come to dwell in the body of a human being. And "in the body of the human being the whole of creation finds its crossroads and unification"—thus "the whole cosmos is involved in what happened in the body of Christ."[40]

And He Awaits Fulfillment

All of this has taken place in the human body of Christ in anticipation of all things being gathered up in him, the things in heaven and those on earth, in the fullness of time (Ephesians 1:9ff.).

Chapter 42

Methodological Principles IV

The Strata of the Gospels

The entire Bible is the word of God, and this being the case, we should follow certain general guidelines when we read it. Nevertheless, the Bible is composed of parts with different characteristics that call for a particular methodology. Some guidelines for reading the gospels follow.

In this regard, the so-called "form critical" method comes to mind (also known as *Formgeschichte,* literally, "history of forms"), a method that seeks to explain the origin of the gospels by retracing their textual development. It stems from the work of the Protestant scholars Debelius and Bultmann and has stimulated continuing widespread discussion.

Pre-existing Literary Units in the Early Christian Community

The method in question considers the body of the gospels as it has come down to us and seeks to pinpoint some smaller literary units, such as collections of maxims or narratives of miracles, that might have preceded it. These units would have formed the nucleus from which the gospels would later be developed in the form we know today. Questions concerning the date and location of the creation of these literary units are raised to ascertain their origin.

The answers given to these questions usually suggest that these smaller units sprung up in the early Christian communities. According to the form critical method, these communities resembled their contemporary popular culture and were thus somewhat similar to all communities of all times and places, the anonymous crowds from which legends arise. Popular cultures are not concerned with history in the true sense of the word. The Christian community in particular was enlivened by the memory of the earthly life of Jesus and their awaiting his return. What enlivened it was faith, and faith—as it is said—is creative in some way. A historian who wants to trace the "authentic" kernel of the life of Jesus must work at stripping the gospels of what the popular imagination is supposed to have added from the realm of myth and legend. This work must be done by comparing the related bodies of contemporary literature, such as Hellenistic and rabbinic literature.

A Critique of "Form Criticism"

Many of the tenets of form criticism are simply unfounded. First of all, the primitive Christian community bears no resemblance to an anonymous crowd; instead, it is an organized community with leadership. For one thing, the apostles carefully restore the number of their group to twelve after Jesus' ascension, with a prominent position occupied by Peter. The apostles proclaim a precise message: Christ died on the cross and rose again. Their proclamation in no way resembles a mythical invention. They refer to the prehistory of Christ as found in the Old Testament and state that they are eyewitnesses of what they recount. The apostles are not interested in fabricating the figure of Christ; rather, they seek to corroborate the historical truth of his person, his mission, and especially his death and resurrection, all of which form the foundations of faith.

The "Instruction": The Three Phases of the Gospels

The Pontifical Biblical Commission clarified the issue with an instruction, published April 21, 1964, which was taken up in the Dogmatic Constitution on Divine Revelation (*Dei verbum*, 18–19). First of all, it confirmed the historical truth of the gospels, which "faithfully convey what Jesus, Son of God, during his life among men, effectively did and taught for their eternal salvation, until the day he ascended to heaven." It went on to identify three phases through which the gospels passed:

1. Jesus' own preaching

2. The apostles' preaching
   After having been enlightened by the glorious events of Christ and the Holy Spirit, and having acquired a deeper and fuller understanding of these events, the apostles then preached. Therefore, the gospels transmit to us the preaching of Jesus, not exactly as the apostles received it in the very moment Jesus was preaching, but as those words were filtered through the fulfillment of the events and through the apostles' own enlightenment by the Holy Spirit. In some passages the evangelists point out that certain occurrences were not really understood until later on (for example, John 2:21ff.). In this way, a vast heritage of traditions gradually forms around the words and actions of Jesus, which are first transmitted orally.

3. The evangelists' writings
   In their writing the evangelists choose from among this vast wealth of material. They gather and synthesize it, drawing attention to certain facts according to their personal interest and to the needs of the particular audience to whom their writings were addressed. (See, for example, Matthew 1:1ff., which is intended for Jewish believers. Here, Matthew cites the genealogy of Jesus in order to establish his connection to David and Abraham, who are key figures in the history of Israel. The gospel of Luke, however, is addressed to Gentiles and traces the genealogy of Jesus to Adam [Luke 2:3ff.], because in Adam are included all people, not just the Jews.) Therefore, the evangelists adapt the material they are recounting according to the capacities and needs of their readers, "always, however, in such a way as to reflect on Jesus with sincerity and truthfulness."

These three stages in the formation of the gospels are also affirmed in *Dei verbum,* 19. Accordingly, below are some practical guidelines that can facilitate the reading of the gospels.

A Theological Purpose and a Historical Basis

It is important to avoid the tendency to consider the sayings of Jesus contained in the evangelists' texts as if they were recorded verbatim, and to view the narratives as if they were journalistic reporting. Like the Old Testament, the gospels come to us from a time and a setting that are quite distant from our own. Also, the criteria involved in their compilation differ greatly from modern ones. Their aim is theological, but it must be remembered that faith in both Judaism and Christianity is historical. If the gospels are not historical texts, they could not be the basis for theological statements. The inspired theological reflection that gave rise to the gospels could not stray from the historical truth of the events without rendering itself null and void.

In the gospels, as in the Old Testament, it is important to consider the intention of the author, but without doing so too hastily. It may be useful to compare the evangelists among themselves—to explore the literary genre, the manner of speaking common to their environment—keeping in mind, for example, that certain sayings would have been repeated by Jesus himself often and on different occasions, with their form varying somewhat.

It is perhaps unnecessary to note the deep and reverent feelings that the evangelical texts arouse in each Christian who comes in contact with them. They contain what the apostles, inspired by the Holy Spirit, wrote down after having preached the same thing. They constitute the "foundation of our faith" (*Dei verbum*, 18).

Chapter 43

The Annunciation

Mary's "Yes"

In the determining moment of salvation history, God once again seeks a human being to collaborate with him in the execution of the divine plan through a freely given assent to his will. This moment of history begins when Mary responds to the words of the angel, the messenger of God's greatest gift, by saying, "Let it be with me according to your word" (Luke 1:38). As with all the events of the history of salvation, this event springs from a gift of God and from the assent given to this gift by the creature.

The Faith of Mary and the Faith of Abraham

"Let it be done with me according to your word" is the continuation of a chain of positive responses to God's call, from Abraham to Moses—even though his response was given somewhat hesitantly—to David, who had "stayed behind to tend the flock." Like Abraham, Mary believes in God as the source of life, the one who can cause life to spring forth in circumstances that are impossible from a human perspective. In this vein Guardini says,

> The attitude of faith that is required of Mary is primarily the faith of the Old Testament. Since what is in question—namely, redemption—has yet to be fulfilled, to believe is to make oneself available for the realization of this event.[41]

Like Abraham, Mary believes in a promise which consists of the gift of life under conditions that seem to be totally negative.

The Divine Motherhood

Once again, where the gift of God meets with faith and welcome on the part of the creature, life springs forth. Mary thus becomes a Mother in the most extraordinary circumstances: She becomes the Mother of Jesus Christ, the Son of God. Her divine motherhood is, first of all, the totally transforming reception of the Holy Spirit into herself. This reception occurs through faith; her motherhood has its true beginnings in a religious act of submission and openness to the gift of God, which precedes the biological phenomenon. Accordingly, Saint Augustine notes,

> The same blessed Virgin conceived believing in whom she delivered while believing. In fact, upon being promised a child, and having asked how this could happen . . . she received the angel's reply: "The Holy Spirit will descend upon you . . ." When the angel said this, she, who was filled with faith, conceived Christ, first in her mind, then in her womb: "Let it be done to me according to your word," she replies.[42]

Elsewhere he adds, "Indeed, the maternal relationship would have been of no advantage to Mary had she not borne Jesus more happily in her heart than in her flesh."[43] All these texts can be understood as a commentary on the words of Elizabeth, "Blessed is she who believed that there would be a fulfillment of what was spoken to her by the Lord" (Luke 1:45).[44]

Therefore, the angel's words herald an event that continues and carries forth the history of Israel and yet is at the same time a completely new event. The very wording of the angel's announcement points to the continuity of this event regarding past history as well as to the newness that this event brings to the history.

Prophetic Announcements and the Annunciation

Throughout the history of Israel, when the prophets announce the coming of the Messiah, they usually deliver their message in a three-part structure. First they invite the person (or people) to rejoice:

Sing aloud, O daughter Zion,
Shout, O Israel!
Rejoice and exult with all your heart,
O daughter Jerusalem! (Zephaniah 3:14)

Second, they go on to explain that the cause of joy is the presence of God: "The Lord, your God, is in your midst" (Zephaniah 3:17). Finally, they often add an invitation not to be afraid: "Do not fear" (Zephaniah 3:16, see also Joel 2:21–22).

In Luke's gospel (1:28) the angel greets Mary with the word *khaire,* which has been rendered "hail" ("greetings") in English, but its true meaning is "rejoice." Immediately afterward the angel adds, "The Lord is with you." The third element of prophetic announcements lies in verse 30: "Do not be afraid."

Thus, the angel's words are meant as a continuation and a seal of the words the prophets used throughout the centuries to announce God's promise of salvation to Israel. That salvation is a child to whom will be given the name "Jesus," the Savior.[45]

The Virgin Birth

While the Incarnation is a continuation of the history preceding it, it is also a completely new event. As Karl Rahner has written,

> The birth of this Son through no human paternal intervention and yet through a true reproductive process within a mother signifies that, with this event, a radically new point of departure is established in salvation history. The history of humankind encumbered by sin does not continue, but is renewed in Redemption.[46]

Tertullian had already written, "Why did Jesus have to be born from a Virgin? It was necessary that the One who brought the gift of new birth be born in a new way."[47]

The Immaculate Conception

The birth of Christ from Mary represents something totally new in the reproduction of human beings for another and even more important reason. Jesus is borne by a creature who was not affected by sin. Mary benefited from redemption more than any other creature. Mary's acceptance of Christ is an event of such radical importance that redemption acts upon her differently than on other creatures; it acts for her preservation. Because she was born free from original sin, Mary can offer a dwelling in her womb that is worthy of Christ.

At the point of convergence between the Old and New Testaments, Mary bears in herself the one who, through his blood, will seal the new and eternal covenant. On the threshold of the new times, when a new humanity is about to come forth, Mary stands as its champion in her full reception of Christ into herself and in her offering of him as a gift to the world.

It has been said that Mary is the first realization of the perfect Christian.

> If Christianity is, in its fullest form, the pure acceptance of the salvation of God who is One and Three and is revealed in Jesus Christ, then Mary is the perfect Christian. She is the totally Christian human being, because in her faith, her spirit, and in her womb—which is to say, with her body and her soul and all the power of her being—she received and welcomed the eternal Word of the Father. . . . If to be a Christian means that one's own grace shines forth and reverberates in selfless service for the salvation of others, then Mary is the perfect example. With the assent of her faith and in the physical concreteness of her divine motherhood she received the One who is the salvation of all, Jesus Christ, our Lord.[48]

Chapter 44

The Birth of Jesus

Bethlehem

The very choice of the place for Jesus' birth is significant: Bethlehem is the birthplace of David, who, according to the biblical tradition, is one of the principal prototypes of the Messiah. Furthermore, the prophet Micah (5:1ff.) explicitly compares the smallness of the town—"But you, O Bethlehem of Ephrathah, who are one of the little clans of Judah"—with the grandeur of the event that would occur there: "From you shall come forth for me one who is to rule in Israel, whose origin is from of old, from ancient days."

The grandeur of the event is such that Matthew, who writes *post eventum*, quotes the words of the prophet. However, in doing so, he can no longer see Bethlehem as "one of the little clans of Judah"; instead, he states, "You . . . are by no means least among the rulers of Judah" (Matthew 2:6).

The Announcement to the Shepherds

The prophetic text emphasizes a contrast that is found repeatedly in the evangelists' narratives concerning the birth of Jesus. This contrast is also evident in the words of the angels who bring the announcement to the shepherds at Bethlehem: "Do not be afraid. I bring you news of great joy."

The Child Is the Messiah, the Lord

Joy is the effect of the presence of God among people: "Today in the town of David a savior has been born to you; he is Christ the Lord." Here the mystery of Christ is revealed in all its grandeur: He is the Messiah, the long-awaited one who would bring salvation. He is the Lord, the *Kyrios,* the title that the Old Testament jealously reserves for God alone. Immediately after this grand statement we read, "You will find a child wrapped in bands of cloth and lying in a manger" (Luke 2:10ff.). Even more simply, Matthew writes, "She gave birth to a son; and [Joseph] named him Jesus" (Matthew 1:25, paraphrased).

About Whom the Prophets Spoke

Even the structure of the angel's words, which recall the style of prophetic announcements, contributes to the opening of vast historical perspectives concerning the birth of this child and points to the convergence of the history of Israel in this event. Matthew notes in regard to the virgin birth, "Now all this took place to fulfill the words spoken by the Lord through the prophet." He says the same thing in reference to the choice of the birthplace (2:6), the flight into Egypt (2:15), the lamenting of the mothers following the massacre of the innocents (2:18), and the fact that Jesus was called "the Nazarene" (2:23). The whole history was waiting for the first cry of this Child.

In addition, all the Gentiles, represented by the Magi, proceed to his cradle, around which choirs of angels and heavenly hosts are descending and exulting. All of these details are of the deepest theological significance. The Incarnation is an event that, though prepared and brought to maturation in Israel, affects the whole of humankind. Therefore, around the cradle of Jesus Christ there could not have been only Jewish shepherds giving homage; all of humankind has to be present.

The Peoples of the Earth Gather around Him

Indeed, the Magi "saw the child with Mary his mother; and they knelt down and paid him homage" (Matthew 2:11).

In his commentary on Matthew's gospel,[49] W.F. Albright points out how the literature of the early Christian era attests to the importance of the Magi as professional astrologers. They were known to have traveled all around the Mediterranean and were sought out and listened to in the marketplace as well as at court. Since the messianic movement was afoot, it is very likely that, in his preoccupation with possible usurpers of his power, Herod would have wanted to consult with the Magi. The appearance of signs in the heavens on the occasion of important events, hence, on the birth of an important personage, is also attested to in classical literature.[50]

It is noteworthy that the announcement is given to the Jewish people in their listening to the words of the heavenly messenger. (Listening is the particular stance of the Jewish people; thus, God makes himself known to them through direct communication.) The same announcement is given to the Gentiles in their observation of nature.

And the Heavens Are Stirred

That small baby's body is the body of the Word of God. Thus, he is not only the ruler of humankind but the ruler of the angels, who can not keep from singing their song around him. Furthermore, the fact that a human body—which by its very nature is linked to the material cosmos— has become the temple of God on earth cannot but reverberate in the subhuman world. Indeed, extraordinary manifestations of the Savior's birth appear in the nonhuman world, among them a star to point the way to his birthplace.

Because the Child Is God and Human

The dual nature of the events surrounding the birth of Christ—of both extreme humility and striking grandeur—points to the dual nature of this baby who is born to humankind. He is like any other baby born into this world, and yet he is immeasurably different from any other creature.

In the gospel of Matthew the uniqueness of the event in the unfolding history of salvation is lifted up in the opening words, "An account of the genealogy of Jesus the Messiah, the son of David, the son of Abraham" (1:1). Jesus is immediately introduced to us as the heir to the messianic promise and is therefore linked to the previous history of Israel, from its inception with the first patriarch. But there is more here. Matthew's opening line, "The book of the genealogy . . ." recalls a particular phrase which recurs twice in the Old Testament. In Genesis 5 there is a kind of summary of creation, "This is the book of the generations of Adam. When God created man, he made him in the likeness of God. . . . When Adam had lived a hundred and thirty years, he became the father of a son, in his own likeness, after his image" (Genesis 5:1ff.). The history of humankind begins when God imprints his image in a creature, which is then carried forth through the transmission of the image from parent to child.

Jesus' Birth Is Traced to the Inception of the World

The correspondence between the two passages in Matthew and Genesis is striking in view of the rarity of the opening phrase. Matthew wrote for a Jewish audience, which was undoubtedly familiar with the book of Genesis and for whom the gospel passage would naturally connect to that of the Old Testament. Hence, the birth of Jesus was traced back in time and connected to the birth of Adam. This is a way of specifying the universality of the event, which is rooted in the history of Israel, yet exceeds these boundaries in its connection to the birth of Adam, thus involving all of humankind. Jesus' birth is a cosmic event which ripples out to all creation, infusing it with new life.

Jesus' Birth Inaugurates a Generation of New Human Beings

Although the birth of Christ can be traced to the beginnings of the world, it is more importantly an event that heralds the dawn of a totally new era in history. The genealogy of Adam—which is a genealogy of the life of the flesh—consists of the list of his descendants up to Jesus. When the genealogy stops with Jesus, we can't help but wonder where the descendants of Jesus are. With Jesus' arrival, does the unfolding of history come to a halt, reversing its direction toward the past? By means of flesh, Adam transmitted the image of God to his children and grandchildren. What about Jesus, born of Mary and called the Christ (Matthew 1:16)? With him history pauses, but it is not a "screeching halt" or a shutdown; rather, it is one of those moments when history is charged with new energy and takes off in new directions. From Christ onward, the image of God is no longer transmitted to people through the flesh but through a wholly spiritual reproductive process to those men, women, and children who open themselves to it.

The history continued uninterrupted from the first Adam to Christ, the second Adam. With the second Adam creation is renewed and begins again. Human beings are now given the possibility of being created anew as well, by becoming children of God in Christ.

Chapter 45

The Presentation in the Temple

Just as Israel shared the customs of the peoples of its time and was set apart only because of its particular knowledge of God, so Jesus, who took on human nature in the womb of a specific people, shares all their habits and customs and will be set apart from them only by the absence of sin within him. From the first days of his earthly life he conforms to the religious practices of every pious Israelite. He was circumcised on the eighth day after birth, and then, "when the time came for their purification according to the Law of Moses, they took him up to Jerusalem to present him to the Lord" (Luke 2:22ff.).

The Purification of the Mother

It is important to be aware of an ancient two-part custom in Israel regarding the birth of a child. The first part concerned the newly delivered mother, who must purify herself, because according to the Mosaic Law, she was in a state of legal impurity for seven days after giving birth.

Legal impurity signified a state of incapacity for worship; thus, whoever became impure could not participate in certain activities of worship. These customs were ancient and were linked to the Jews' deep respect toward any manifestation of life forces, which came only from God for Israel. To the seven days of major impurity—during which time the "impure person" could transmit her condition to others—were added thirty-three more days of minor impurity for the new mother. During this time the woman was forbidden to eat meats offered in sacrifice or to go to the Temple (Leviticus 12:1ff.).

On the fortieth day of impurity one had to sacrifice a year-old lamb, a pigeon or a dove. A pair of turtledoves or two young pigeons was a sufficient offering for a poor woman. Mary fulfills this religious obligation by presenting herself at the Temple when the days of her purification are completed.

The Ransom of the Firstborn

In addition to the purification of the mother, Jews had to ransom every firstborn male by offering a lamb (Exodus 34:20), or by paying five shekels (Numbers 18:16). This practice was linked to the death of the Egyptian firstborn males and the sparing of the Jewish firstborn (Exodus 13:13ff.). In gratitude for this event, every firstborn son "who opens the mother's womb" is offered to the Lord in sacrifice; the firstborn of the human race is ransomed. This practice did not require the presence of the child in the Temple, only the payment of the ransom.

In Luke's account of the Presentation, Jesus is taken to the Temple. There is no mention of an offering of a lamb or the payment of five shekels. Luke speaks only of the sacrifice of doves and pigeons, which concern the mother. He says that Jesus was taken to Jerusalem to be presented to the Lord.

The Consecration of Jesus at the Temple

According to Luke's text, then, Jesus is *not* ransomed as would be any other firstborn in Israel. Yet, in not being ransomed he remains consecrated to the Lord. The ransoming of Jesus would have contradicted the very meaning of his life, which was, is, and always will be an offering to the Father.

The presence of Jesus in the Temple is perhaps connected to the ancient story of Samuel, who was taken to the Temple by his mother, not to be ransomed but to be consecrated to the Lord in a definitive way (Samuel 1:24ff.). This connection is further evidenced in Luke's gospel in the examination of the Magnificat, the canticle in which Mary praises God for having allowed her to become the mother of his son, and of the canticle of Hannah (1 Samuel 2:1ff.), the mother of Samuel, in which she expresses her joy and gratitude for experiencing motherhood after a long period without children.

The similarity between the two hymns is well known, and their relationship is particularly clear in the phrase, "for he has looked with favor on the lowliness (humiliation) of his servant" (Luke 1:48). These words, which come from Mary's mouth and are difficult to interpret, are also placed on the lips of Hannah. In Hannah's instance, however, they have a clear meaning: Her barrenness had made her inferior to her husband's other wife.

Apparently Luke, whose gospel is rich in well-structured theology, wants to establish a relationship between Samuel, who is born miraculously from a barren mother and whose birth is considered a particular gift from God, and Jesus, who is born from a virgin and is the priceless gift of God to humankind.

As Samuel is consecrated to God, so Jesus is brought to the Temple in celebration of his most unique consecration to the Father.

Chapter 46

Apostles, Disciples, Scribes, and Pharisees[51]

In the Crowds Surrounding Jesus

During his public life Jesus is surrounded by crowds that gather in large numbers to listen to a Man who speaks "as no one has ever spoken before." Throngs of people press in so close to him that it is difficult to breathe. In following him people even forget to eat. But what is the composition of the crowd?

Apostles

In the foreground are the apostles, whom Jesus chooses for a very particular mission after spending a night in prayer (Luke 6:10ff.). There are also the disciples, seventy-two in number, who are called by Jesus and commissioned to heal the sick and to announce that the Kingdom of God is near. In the gospels they are depicted as being overjoyed when they return from a mission successfully completed (Luke 10:17), and dejected when they fail due to their lack of faith (Matthew 17:14ff.).

Zealots and Herodians

And who are the others crowding around Jesus? They are a more varied lot, including the members of the many contemporary religious movements. There are the Zealots, whose faith was founded on the sword and who did not hesitate to use violence. Their group included the apostle Simon, the one called "the Canaanite" or "the Zealot." There are also the Herodians, who are not as easy to identify. Though not included in the crowds around Jesus, there are also the ascetics of Qumran, who would probably have been part of the Essenes. Their messianic dream had led them away from the city to wait for the Messiah in the desert.

Sadducees

The gospels record some of the arguments between Jesus and the Sadducees, an aristocratic religious group with ties to the levitical priesthood and thus to the Temple. They are open to Hellenistic influences and, at the same time, are hostile to internal changes. For this reason some scholars claim that they refused to accept the authority of the oral tradition and felt bound only to the scriptures. Yet this is incorrect; they were simply antagonistic toward populist innovations and desired to preserve certain privileges for the priestly caste. Furthermore, the Sadducees are distinguished by their position on certain doctrinal concepts, such as the resurrection of the dead and the afterlife, which they deny.

Pharisees and Scribes

This denial of the resurrection of the dead places the Sadducees in opposition to Jesus as well as to the other major religious group of the time, the Pharisees, who are often named alongside the scribes in the gospels. Although the scribes and Pharisees are two separate groups, they converge at a common point of interest that is of fundamental importance: the Torah (the Law). The scribes are scholars of the Torah; the Pharisees represent the masses who scrupulously comply with its practical, everyday applications. This does not preclude the fact that many scribes might also be Pharisees—that is, devotees of the Law, both in their work as scholars and in the application of its rules and regulations.

Of the various religious movements at the time of Christ, only the Pharisees will survive the destruction of the Temple and the Jewish state by the Roman legions.

The Sadducees, bound to the Temple, disappear along with it, as do other religious movements of lesser importance.

The Spirituality of the Pharisees

The vitality of the Pharisaic movement stemmed from its being the source of a new spirituality in Israel. The Pharisees freed themselves from ties to the Temple as well as to the priests. Their spirituality was no longer centered on blood sacrifices but found an alternative in a different kind of worship, one that focused on the Torah and a prayerful response to it.

The Scriptures and Prayer

Israel was able to survive even the destruction of the Temple on the Mount Zion in Jerusalem because, for quite some time, it had already been acknowledged that "the sacrifice of the lips"—prayer—is more pleasing to the Lord than blood sacrifice (Hosea 14:2). In the period leading up to the destruction of the Temple, the priestly order was being discredited and the very institution of the priesthood called into question, because it had fallen into the hands of inept and unworthy leadership. At the same time, the laity began to express the need for a religious practice that would be accessible to the entire priestly people of Israel. The Pharisees pointed out that it is not the blood sacrifices that render Israel worthy in the eyes of the Lord, but the Torah. The tribes of Israel, they said, are more precious to the Lord than the priests; furthermore, any individual, even a heathen, who is interested in the Law is equal to the high priest in the Lord's eyes.

The Synagogue

Springing up alongside the Temple—and somewhat in opposition to it—was the Synagogue, the institution that concretized the new spirituality. Synagogue worship included proclaiming the word of God and praying. In the Synagogue the exercise of worship was open to everyone—unlike the Temple, where only Israelites of the priestly tribe could officiate. Thus, the Synagogue met the new needs of the masses.

The origin of the Synagogue and its spirituality date to the time of the Babylonian exile (586–536 BCE) when, with the destruction of the Temple, Israel found itself in a foreign land—an impure land—and was unable to worship God with blood sacrifice. Hence, Israel focused its religious life on the only possession it had managed to preserve and bring into exile: the traditions of the patriarchs. However, this spirituality was not contingent upon exile; once the Israelites returned to the land of their ancestors, this spirituality was deepened and diffused.

A Popular and Holistic Spirituality

The spirituality of the Pharisees can be defined as a popular spirituality: It belonged to the people. It called every Israelite to become aware of his or her religious nature. It was also a holistic spirituality: It required that the whole of one's life—every instant of it—be enlivened through obedience to the Law. Everything belongs to God; thus, each detail of one's life must be given as an offering. Nothing may be held back.

The symbolic number of the precepts that are meant to direct the life of a Jew is 613—the sum of the days of the year (365) plus the number of parts that Jewish tradition says the human body has (248). This means that no day may pass without one's being engaged in the observance of the Law, and that one must adhere to the Law with one's whole being.

Its Seed of Danger

The spirituality of the Pharisees was a very "high-level" spirituality, one that aimed at God's sovereign rule over the entire community and every instant of each individual life. Yet, this did not prevent Pharisaic spirituality—like everything else in this world—from carrying a seed of danger, one that was hidden in the very excellence of such piety.

As noted, for the Pharisees the Torah was the object of the greatest veneration. In their view, no human being had the authority to subject it to evaluation or to prioritize its contents. The Torah is the word of God and the expression of God's will. It could not be debated. "Neither can a corpse contaminate it, nor water purify it," say the rabbis, "unless so decreed by the King of Kings." Against the backdrop of the Pharisaic veneration of the Law, we discover the grandeur of the God of the prophets.

But the deep veneration of the Torah can be lost in legalistic minutiae. Hence, Jesus reprimanded the Pharisees for tying the prescribed practice more to the letter of the Law than to the spirit of the Scriptures.

These reprimands were well founded, yet they strike at the subversion of a spirituality that is worthy of great respect in itself, because it is based on the highest veneration of God's word. The Jews themselves were aware of this subversion, and—as is evident in the Jewish post-biblical texts—they attacked Pharisaic spirituality with irony and sarcasm.

The Parable of the Pharisee

The parable of the Pharisee and the tax collector (Luke 18:9ff.) points out the two most serious dangers present in pharisaic spirituality.

The Pharisee boasts of the works he has performed: "I thank you, God, that I am not grasping, unjust, adulterous like the rest of humankind, and particularly that I am not like this tax collector here. I fast twice a week; I pay tithes on all I get." By enumerating his works and rejoicing in them, he forgets the work of God in him that enables him to do such works. Thus the man's position before God is distorted. Conscious of the importance of his works, he feels empowered to present God with a list of his good deeds, almost to the point of demanding reciprocity. The benefits God has bestowed upon him are no longer graciously received as gifts, but are viewed as things due him, things he has rightfully earned because of his good deeds.

Human beings do not stand before God in a relationship of give and take. To God we give nothing; from God we receive everything. With God we do not have credits, only debits; yet God's mercy gives us hope that our debts will be remitted.

Second, one who is continuously preoccupied with his or her adherence to detailed precepts may easily come to value the works in themselves, independently from God's work within himself or herself, and independently from the Spirit that enables him or her to do the work in the first place. For instance, in the parable the Pharisee claims to have restrained himself from greediness and adultery; he has fasted and paid his tithe; but he is not concerned with ridding his heart of conceit and contempt for his fellow human beings. The good deed itself is only material and lacks the proper spirit. Fasting observed without love signifies no more than a little less food consumed. Tithes paid with a heart full of conceit are but lifeless metal coins. Food and metal can have meaning only if accompanied by the spiritual fervor of the one making the fast or paying the tithe.

Such a separation between the works themselves and the spirit in which they are performed results in a division within the human being. On one side is the action; on the other side the spirit, which can be totally disconnected from the action. This was pharisaic spirituality's undoing; religious integrity, the holistic spirituality that formed its very base, was destroyed. It is here that the conflict between Jesus and the Pharisees is clearest, for Jesus indeed demands a total unity of heart and action.

A Universal Human Figure

The parable of the Pharisee and the tax collector points out the state of deterioration into which pharisaic spirituality had fallen in Jesus' time. However, it also refers to people of all times and places, since pharisaism is a universal phenomenon. Jesus' preaching is not addressed only to Jews, nor is the Pharisee depicted in the parable necessarily Jewish; rather, he is a universal human figure in whom each of us can recognize at least a part of ourselves.

The Pharisees tend to get singled out in the gospels as stubborn antagonists to Jesus. They are the ones with whom the Teacher willingly argues. Yet this is only part of the truth. Without a doubt, the Pharisees were sharply criticized by Jesus, and there were even intense clashes between them; nevertheless, the gospels also attest to the fact that the relations between Jesus and the Pharisees were not always combative. Why did Jesus often sit at the same table and share a meal with them (Luke 7:36; 11:37; 14:1)? How was it that he could continuously preach in the synagogue?

Jesus recognizes the authority of the scribes and Pharisees when he acknowledges that they occupy the chair of Moses and exhorts the people to follow their precepts, even though "they do not practice what they teach." He affirms their teaching with regard to certain prescribed offerings: "Therefore, do whatever they teach you and follow it" (Matthew 23:3). Like the Pharisees, Jesus wears a fringed robe (Mark 6:56) as prescribed by the Law (Numbers 15:38; Deuteronomy 22:12) and demands

observance of the rules that forbid the use of the Temple, a place consecrated to the Lord, as a shortcut when transporting profane objects. His
way of arguing, his very preaching in parables makes him similar to the
rabbis and leads one to believe that, among the religious groups of his
time, Jesus most closely resembles the Pharisees in their most positive
attributes. His clashes with them probably result from the frequent con-
tacts that such a closeness dictated.[52]

Chapter 47

The Preaching of Jesus and Worship in the Synagogue[53]

The Gospels indicate that Jesus attended the Synagogue regularly and that he preached there many times, thus inserting his message into the framework of synagogue worship (Matthew 4:23; 12:9; 13:54; Mark 1:21ff.; John 18:20). This happened so frequently that there must be a particular reason for it; hence, a closer look at the worship of the Synagogue is warranted.

The Structure of Worship in the Synagogue

As we know, the focal point of worship in the Synagogue is the reading of the Torah (the Pentateuch). Early on—and certainly by the time of Jesus—a second reading was added, taken from the books of the prophets. In texts dated a little after the time of Jesus—which probably reflect the practices of Jesus' time—the passage from the prophets serves primarily to aid the explanation of the Law. It may offer some historical note or a spiritual commentary to the feast of the day. There were also prophetic readings of a messianic character, which described future times or the deliverer who would come "in that day" to bring prosperity, salvation, and abundance of God's spirit to his people.

Messianic Character

The prophetic reading followed the first reading and projected it toward the future by stirring the hearer's spirit toward the expectation of an event—or, better, a person—that was yet to come. Thus, the liturgy of the Synagogue appears to have been a worship entirely geared toward something awaiting fulfillment.

This spirituality of hope found its best expression in the prayer which served as the response to the readings, the Kaddish. This prayer is predominantly messianic in character, and its similarities to the "Our Father" are obvious:

> May his great name be magnified and sanctified,
> in the world he created according to his will.
> May his kingdom come during your life,
> and in your days and during the life of all
> the house of Israel, soon and very soon.

Reading the promises of God stimulated the desire that these promises would soon be realized, and this desire was lifted up in prayer.

Jesus preached his message against this backdrop; in such a setting he could find hearts poised to accept his word. The worship in the Synagogue awakened hearts to hope; Jesus responded by revealing himself to be the fulfillment of this hope. Many of the episodes in Jesus' life cannot be fully understood unless viewed in this light.

The Parable of the Good Shepherd

For example, Jesus told the parable of the Good Shepherd (John 10 ff.) on the occasion of the feast of the Dedication, the feast that commemorated the purification of the Temple by Judas the Maccabee after its profanation at the hands of Antiochus Epiphanes.

The subject of the parable seems to have been suggested to Jesus by the synagogue readings for that day. According to an ancient source, the liturgy for the Dedication called for the reading of passages whose central topic was always the "shepherd,"[54] such as Genesis 46:28ff., in which the brothers of Joseph, the leaders of the twelve tribes of Israel, are presented as shepherds since childhood; the first book of Samuel, which contains the deeds of the shepherd David, who protects his sheep from wild animals; and Ezekiel 34:1ff., in which David is the "one shepherd" whom the Lord will appoint to watch over his sheep when he makes a "covenant of peace" with them. This feast, then, offered an opportunity for Jesus to present himself as the Good Shepherd, the antithesis of those shepherds who, as Ezekiel points out, fed only themselves. The Good Shepherd, who defends his sheep against the wolf and lays down his life for the sheep, repeats the deeds of David and, like David, is the one shepherd appointed by the Lord to tend his flock. He is that shepherd who, like the Lord himself in the Ezekiel passage, has the utmost love for his sheep and goes out to search for the lost. Thus, the figure of the Good Shepherd stands out against the backdrop of the Old Testament, and the parable becomes an explicit messianic declaration by Jesus.

"Let Anyone Who Is Thirsty Come to Me"

The preaching of Jesus mirrors another great Jewish festival, the autumnal festival. The Pharisees had introduced elements of a popular nature into the Temple liturgy for this feast, particularly the pouring of water on the altar in the concluding phase of the festival. Water was drawn from outside the walls of Jerusalem and brought into the city through the so-called "Water Gate." The water was poured on the altar to ask God's favor in the form of rain; however, the prophetic readings gave this ritual a messianic interpretation:

> On that day living waters shall flow out from Jerusalem, half of them to the eastern sea and half of them to the western sea; it shall continue in summer as in winter. And the Lord will become king over all the earth; on that day the Lord will be one and his name one (Zechariah 14:8–9).

These words urged the people not to dwell on the present, but to see in those waters being poured on the altar the perennial living waters that "on that day" would make the earth fertile. Ezekiel 47:1ff. also speaks of abundant, life-giving waters that would restore and enliven all living beings.

Against this backdrop Jesus' cry is heard: "Let anyone who is thirsty come to me, and let the one who believes in me drink" (John 7:37). Jesus does not proclaim these words at some random moment; rather, he waits for the moment when hearts are turned toward messianic hope and are poised in expectation and longing for its fulfillment, the moment when hearts are most receptive. The inexhaustible source of living water is present, and his water is the source of eternal life.

The Discourse on the "Bread of Life"

Another of Jesus' discourses is clearest when viewed against the back-drop of the paschal festival. In the synagogue at Capernaum, after multi-plying the bread, Jesus delivers his homily on the bread of life as a commentary on the miracle. The starting point for this discourse can be found in the words with which the Jewish crowd argues with Jesus: "What sign are you going to give us then, so that we may see it and believe you? What work are you performing? Our ancestors ate the manna in the wilderness; as it is written, 'He gave them bread from heaven to eat'" (John 6:30–31).

The evangelist's text does not make any reference to the liturgy of the day, assuming that it is widely known. However, it is not clear to the modern reader why the crowd would bring up the miracle of the manna or what causes the discussion to get started in the first place. All this becomes clearer if, as seems to be the case, those in the synagogue have just listened to the reading of the passage in Numbers 11, which contains the account of the manna in the desert. The people give Jesus the oppor-tunity with their question to show how a miracle of long ago is in ful-filled in him.

In this way, Jesus constantly inserts his message into the context of Jewish worship. He does so from the beginning of his public life in the Synagogue at Nazareth (Luke 4:14ff.), when he solemnly proclaims his messianic mission.

Chapter 48

Preaching the Kingdom of God: The Parables

Jesus' primary teaching method is the telling of parables. The evangelists report a great number of parables, noting that Jesus used them to teach many things (Matthew 13). Moreover, Matthew states that Jesus would never speak to the crowds except in parables (13:34).

The Pedagogy of the Parables

What is particular to the parable as a method of teaching? What is its merit, its didactic value? Its merit lies in the fact that the parable *hides* the truth it wants to teach. Claiming that the merit of a pedagogical system is that it hides the concept it seeks to teach may seem strange. It is usually assumed that a good teacher is one who is capable of presenting to his or her students the whole truth, well displayed and thoroughly delineated from beginning to end.

Such an assumption overlooks the fact that there are two moments in the learning process. The first moment is the one in which the student listens to the teacher in a passive, receptive state; the second is when the student ponders what the teacher has given, reflects upon it, and gradually makes it his or her own. In this second moment the student is no longer a passive listener; rather, the student now utilizes all of his or her personal faculties in order to claim what has been offered. The importance of the second moment is obvious: It is the moment when what has been received by the mind gradually filters down to the depths of the person and slowly becomes the "flesh and blood" of one's spirit.

The first moment would be thwarted and incomplete without the second because it would remain somehow external to the whole person. The student's intellect might be engaged, but a person consists of more than an intellect. Missing the second moment would indicate a lack of a personal work, which is the only way one arrives at a deep acquisition of knowledge.

Furthermore, if in presenting the topic to be studied, the teacher offers all the necessary conclusions, the student will not feel compelled to personal research. What is there to seek when the teacher has already revealed everything? In this case, the student will readily shut down in the first moment of learning, the moment of passive listening, which does not engage one in an active and personal work.

The method of hiding the truth in parables aims precisely at calling the listener to this sort of work in order to lead him or her to true knowledge, a knowledge that is deep and personal. It is in this way that one comes to truly own what he or she has received.

Jesus used parables to teach the greatest mysteries of God, presenting the mystery as if it were a jewel in a treasure box. He doesn't reveal the jewel; he just gives us the box in which it is kept. The box hides the jewel, yet it simultaneously alerts us to the fact that the treasure is hidden inside and invites us to unwrap it in order to claim it. Likewise, the parable hides the truth while simultaneously revealing it; the parable indicates to us where and how we must search out the truth. The truth stands behind the image, behind the "lowly fact" in the parable; the image and the "lowly fact" become guides that lead us to the possession of the truth. In other words, Jesus provides his listeners with the tools needed for personal meditation that can lead to knowledge of the truth. He does not find the treasure for us but leaves to us the compelling work of the search and the joy of progressive discovery. Through the parables, Jesus helps us meditate on our own.

Parables and Liturgical "Signs"

The parables exhibit characteristics similar to liturgical signs. If Saint Augustine could say of a liturgical sign (for example, the bread and wine of the Eucharist, the water of baptism, and so on), *"Aliud videtur, aliud intelligitur"* ("one thing is seen; another is intended"), then we can say of the parable, *"Aliud auditur, aliud intelligitur"* ("one thing is heard; another is intended"). As for the liturgical sign, if one stops at the external reality without seeing the supernatural one hidden within, the world of liturgy would remain closed. Likewise, if one is unable to reach the mystery that the parables conceal, the spirit contained and hidden therein, then it would be completely useless to read and ponder them.

Liturgical "signs" and parables are two aspects of the divine methodology that require a material, perceivable element in order to communicate the *mysterion,* and thus to mediate our reception of knowledge. In itself, the *mysterion* is beyond sensory perception; in order to be perceivable by human beings, it needs a body. The liturgical signs and the parables are such a body.

Parables in the Jewish World

One might ask whether Jesus was the inventor of the literary genre of the parable so characteristic of his preaching. This question is difficult to answer. The rabbis trace the origin of the parable to the time of Solomon. They speak of the parable as being like a deep well with sweet, fresh waters. However, no one could drink because the waters were too far down. They go on to say that a man came and tied ropes together and managed to draw out those waters, so that everyone after him could draw out the waters and quench their thirst. That man was Solomon, who, word by word, parable by parable, at last arrived at the heart of the Torah.

Without pretending to resolve this question, we will limit ourselves to the assertion that since around the time of Christ—or somewhat later—Jewish literature has been rich in parables. Like Jesus, the rabbis also love to "hide" their teachings behind the narrative of brief, imaginary stories. The gospels and rabbinic literature often share common themes: God is a king who has either a field, a garden (the world) or a palace (the Temple, the earth); he has a son (Israel); he hires laborers, and so on. There are many examples, and the same formal elements are adapted to different teachings or the same basic truths are expressed differently in different places. Hence, it appears that there could have existed a common heritage of images and folktales from which both Jesus and the Jewish scholars drew freely, each making suitable adaptations according to his particular teaching.

Thus, the parables are a precious doctrinal heritage in which Jesus "has hidden" the greater part of his teaching and which bring us more deeply into the world of the Teacher who spoke. From a religious perspective, this world differs profoundly from the western world. It approaches divine mystery with great respect. Rather than explaining the mystery, it prefers to conceal it; thus, the human being is invited on a journey of meditation and search, a search that goes always farther and deeper.

Chapter 49

Preaching the Kingdom of God: The Miracles

The Miracles of Jesus

Jesus enacts miracles in relation to things, to nature, and to persons. The miracles are manifestations of his power at all levels of nature, revealing his dominion over all creation. With his voice he calms the storms, giving rise to the question: "What sort of man is this, that even the winds and the sea obey him?" (Matthew 8:27). Inanimate objects obey him; loaves of bread are multiplied; he can even command illness and death to release their prey.

"Repent, for the kingdom of God is at hand."

These are the programmatic words with which Jesus begins his preaching (Matthew 3:2; 4:17; Mark 1:14). This is the message his disciples are to carry throughout the land (Matthew 10:8): the coming near of the kingdom in its completeness, the coming near of the kingdom which completely corresponds to how God wants it to be.

There are basically two instruments Jesus uses in making this announcement: his preaching, particularly the parables, and his miracles. The Second Vatican Council document, *On Divine Revelation (Dei Verbum)*, strongly underscores this dual channel through which one can approach the mystery of the kingdom of God:

> This economy of Revelation is realized by deeds and words, which are intrinsically bound up with each other. As a result, the works performed by

God in the history of salvation show forth and bear out the doctrine and realities signified by the words; the words, for their part proclaim the works, and bring to light the mystery they contain.[55]

The Miracles as "Signs"

Jesus uses two languages: one composed of words, the other composed of deeds. But is it really correct to speak of two languages, or should we not say instead that Jesus always used the same language when preaching about the nearness of the kingdom, the one language he had at his disposal: the language of signs? How could one speak of the kingdom of God if not by means of approximations and allusions that simultaneously reveal but also hide the reality?

The miracles of Jesus are "signs"; it is not without reason that John refers to them with this term (*semeja*) in his Gospel. As with every "sign," the miracles consist of a perceivable element that catches one's attention, and yet, as in the case of every "sign," their meaning is not exhausted by the element perceived. Rather, the signs serve as a bridge to touch an invisible reality.

The miracles say the same thing as the parables—"The kingdom of God is at hand"—and they say it by following the same method of concealing the announcement beneath the veil of the sign. Both the parables and the miracles are forms of preaching. The parables preach with the words, while the miracles preach through deeds. The parables tell what the kingdom of God is like; the miracles show what the kingdom of God will be like—without suffering, without hunger, without death. If we want to get a true picture of the kingdom we are awaiting, we must ponder the parables and miracles together.

The parables present the kingdom to us by means of words; the miracles give us glimpses into the kingdom reality. The miracles are like sudden flashes of light that illuminate the reality of the kingdom and allow us to "see" it. As we have said, the language of the parable is one of allusions, referring us to another reality beyond the one being immediately perceived. The parables tell us what "the kingdom of God is *like* . . ."; yet they do not define the kingdom, because the reality of the kingdom far exceeds all the boundaries that any definition would impose. The immensity of this reality calls us to dig and search, and to return constantly to the digging and searching among the *words and deeds* in order to continue discovering their fuller meaning.

What we seek to clarify in this chapter is how both the words and the miraculous deeds share the same nature.

Like the parables, the miracles contain more than what appears to us at first glance. The miracles offer content that overflows its container. In order to slowly comprehend the miracles in all their richness, it is necessary first to consider them, not only in and of themselves, but also in the framework in which they are being realized. And this framework is the globality of the whole history.

This is what Jesus himself did. When John the Baptist sent his disciples to ask Jesus if he was the Messiah or did they have to wait for another, Jesus responded by referring to his miracles:

> Go and tell John what you hear and see: the blind receive their sight, the lame walk, the lepers are cleansed, the deaf hear, the dead are raised . . . . Matthew 11:4–5

These words echo, almost verbatim, the words of the prophet Isaiah:

> Then the eyes of the blind shall be opened, and the ears of the deaf unstopped; then the lame shall leap like a deer and the tongue of the speechless sing for joy. Isaiah 35:5–6

Thus, with his response Jesus is calling attention to more than the miraculous occurrence in the present moment. Along with the prophet Isaiah, he is inviting us to widen our gaze in order to embrace the whole expanse of history. Isaiah's word "then" certainly points to the coming of Jesus, but it also points to the time of history's fulfillment, that time we still await: the Parousia.

Those miracles witnessed by the crowds that gathered around Jesus during his earthly life are incandescent moments in the global plan of salvation. They are points of particular brilliance that help us "see" what the kingdom will be like in the time of its fulfillment.

In order to penetrate the parables, we must first fix our gaze on the actual images Jesus used. Likewise with the miracles, it is crucial that we not forget the geographical place and the particular moment when the miracle occurred. It is only in gazing intently at the mustard seed, or at the yeast which leavens the entire dough, or at the other images Jesus used, that we will gradually enter more deeply into the reality of the kingdom. We must contemplate the seed itself, and we must carefully "watch" the woman mixing the flour and the yeast, but we must not stop there.

It is the same with the miracles. In order to grasp their full weight, we must look closely at how Jesus cures the sick person. We must listen carefully to his voice as he says to the paralytic: "*Stand up, take your mat, and go home*" (Mark 2:11). We must listen to his voice as he turns toward the deaf man and says: "*Ephphatah!*" (Be opened!) (Mark 7:34) and as he commands the wind and stormy sea: "*Peace! Be still!*" (Mark 4:39). We must listen to Jesus when, in a loud voice, he cries out to Lazarus, who is shut up in the tomb, "*Lazarus, come out!*" (John 11:4). We must pay attention to the details of the miracles, never forgetting their historical and geographical setting.

All of this is necessary in order to root the miracles of Jesus in the reality of history and in order to see them in all their concreteness, but we must not stop there. The miraculous event must be like a springboard that propels us toward the time when God's plan will have reached its fulfillment, that time when there will no longer be any trace of suffering and death, that kingdom which is the utter fullness of Life. Every miracle opens out onto a horizon that is far vaster than the Sea of Galilee or the village of Capernaum, and it is to that horizon that our eyes must move, though without failing to first notice the particular place and person involved in Jesus' miraculous deeds. If we neglect this first step, it is unlikely that we will reach the second step or succeed at penetrating the depths of the mystery of God.

In being attentive to both of these "steps," perhaps the sharp outlines and concise contours in which we are accustomed to seeing Jesus might seem less clear to us, and his figure might seem to stand out less clearly against the background. Yet, at the same time, we see how he grows even greater in stature, charged with all the grandeur, vastness, and dynamism of God's plan for history. The miracles themselves will seem less unexpected, less extraordinary—less singular, we could even say less "miraculous"; but, at the same time, they will assume a new grandeur as landmarks in the unfolding plan of God. They will acquire an almost "ordinary" character, but "ordinary" in the context of the utter grandeur of God's plan.

In that lame person who will *leap like a deer*, in that blind person who *reads the words of the book*, in those crowds who were fed abundantly, we already have a vision of how things will be, of how the world *must* be according to the mind of God. The miracles are like windows that already let us glimpse that world, even if it is already still only in the process of becoming the world God envisions.

The miracles are not only a fountain of marvels, but an announcement of hope.

We are living in the time of waiting and of hope.

The light we have seen emanating from the miracles is not a light that was lit only for a brief moment and then immediately extinguished, to be rekindled only in its eschatological fullness. Rather, that light continues to glow in the depths of human history as it runs its course, and it still breaks through and shines forth, most particularly in those signs that we call the sacraments of the Church, which have also been called "the masterworks of God."[56]

The "golden thread" binds together the miracles of Jesus during his earthly life and that which we live today in our Christian life. This is what enables us to perceive—and to live—the strength, and light, and love of God that are still undergirding history and bringing about the full realization of God's plan for salvation: God's covenant with humankind and the entire cosmos.

At Capernaum Jesus spoke to the paralytic with words that resound in the Church right up to today: *"Your sins are forgiven you"* (Luke 5:20). These are the words that free us from our sins today, just as they liberated the paralytic through an act of salvation in which the freeing of his limbs is the outward and visible sign of an even greater freedom.

The prayer Jesus prayed in a deserted place, asking the Father to satisfy the hunger of the crowds, is always present in the Church, expressed with the words: *This is my Body given for you.* Still today Jesus breaks that Bread for all, that Bread which is his very self, in order to satisfy all who hunger for His Word, for His Presence.

The very newness of life that was manifested in the risen body of Christ at dawn on the first Easter Sunday and that had been prepared for and anticipated in those words and *deeds* of Jesus during his earthly life, we continue to live in those sins that call us to respond "Amen"[57] when we stand before the Bread being offered to us with the words "The body of Christ."

We continue to experience the newness of life in those signs that move us, who are baptized in Christ and thus participants in His death and Resurrection, to respond

> We proclaim your Death, O Lord,
> and profess your Resurrection
> until you come again.

Together the miracles are like a prism which, in its various facets, allow us to see how each illuminates the kingdom: *in words, in deeds, in sacramental signs*. In our time of waiting, they show us now—as though in flashes—what the kingdom will be like at that moment when time will be fulfilled and "the earth will be full of the knowledge of the Lord as the waters cover the sea" (Isaiah 11:9).

Chapter 50

Death and Resurrection

The Evangelical Texts

This chapter will offer a brief guide to the reading of the texts recounting the Resurrection, thought by some to be later texts, laden with apocalyptic elements and a developed theory of angels. This line of thinking has led many to view these texts more as theological affirmations than as the narration of a historical event.

Since the Resurrection is the event upon which the Christian faith is founded, the subject is of particular importance. Hence, the work of Antonio Ammassari[58] is very important, as he investigates the texts with great care. Here we shall refer only to his main points.

It cannot be denied that later elements are included in the accounts of the resurrection; yet, it is important to consider whether they might be interspersed with other, older elements. Ammassari has noted that some details point to a dual source within the individual accounts of the resurrection: specifically, there are two indications of time in Matthew 28:1 and Mark 16:2: the women are entrusted with the mission of announcing the resurrection to the "disciples" in Matthew 28:6 and to the "brothers" later in verse 10, two different categories. Likewise, John 20 refers to the "brothers" in verse 17 and to the "disciples" in verse 18. The invitation "Do not be afraid"[59] is repeated in Matthew 28, verses 5 and 10. These repetitions and discrepancies within the same passage cannot be explained except as the result of the combination of multiple texts.

Ammassari questions why the "young man" *(neaniskos)* seen by the women in the tomb (Mark 16:5) is traditionally understood to be an angel. The term "young man" is never used with reference to angels; furthermore, in their capacity as ambassadors of God, angels never sit down. "Never, in the Old Testament or in the New Testament, do angels sit down or are depicted as being seated. It is God and his Messiah who are seated.[60] Also, the young man in Mark's narrative is seated "on the right-hand side." This detail is in no way insignificant and reminds us of the one "at [God's] right hand," the Son of Man, upon whom God has confirmed his power (in reference to the king of Israel in Psalm 80:18).

There is a variant of Mark 16:7 in which words widely believed to have come from the angel appear: "I am going before you to Galilee. There you will see me just as I told you." Jesus himself would have uttered these words.

Finally, there is a literary tradition, which is primarily an iconographic tradition that depicts Jesus as a young man. It has been noted[61] that in ancient Christian iconography—beginning with the oldest representation of Jesus in the house church at Dura Europos (232–256 CE), in the Roman catacombs and sarcophagi—Jesus is depicted as a beardless young man. This is of special interest, since the subjects dealt with in early Christian art always refer to resurrection and the new life offered to humankind. (One is reminded of the many representations of Jonah, of Daniel among the lions, of the resurrection of Lazarus, of the healing of the paralytic, and so on.) Hence, the figure of Jesus as a young man is linked to a tradition that is almost exclusively focused on the Resurrection.

Who is the figure seated on the right-hand side in the tomb then, the one who speaks in the first person? He is the Risen One whom the women meet in the very place where they had placed his dead body. It is directly from his mouth that they receive the mission of proclaiming the event of the Resurrection.

A primitive layer of the Resurrection narrative can be reconstructed from the accounts of Matthew, Mark, and John, in which either Mary Magdalene or a group of women are the first to see Jesus risen and are, therefore, eyewitnesses of the event. The mediation of women is not a novelty in the gospel. This primitive layer was made secondary and interspersed with other elements where it was deemed necessary to find a more authoritative basis for the announcement of the resurrection, an angel.

It might also be said that it was the clearer understanding of the Risen One's identity that led to the introduction of angels. This was done in order to heighten the sense of transcendence that, in the Jewish setting, always intensifies in the period bridging the two testaments. The development of a concept of angels, which is deemed by some scholars to diminish the effectiveness of the texts, could instead be evidence of a developing Christology.

In light of all this, the reading of the resurrection texts can be approached by searching for the earliest layer. Mark 16:6 seems to be inserted into the text and is similar to words that might be addressed to pilgrims paying a visit to the sepulchre. Supposing this to be the case, the original text would be made up of verses 1–5 and 7–8.

In Matthew 28, which is derived from Mark's gospel, verses 2–8 are more recent and more developed; therefore, after the introductory verse, the narration picks up again at verse 9. Hence, we arrive immediately at the encounter between Jesus and the women. He greets them with the "Rejoice" of the prophetic announcements and with the invitation not to be afraid, as well as with the mission of announcing the event.

In John 20 the narrative of Peter and John's hastening to the tomb has been interwoven with that of the apparition to Mary Magdalene, which begins with the first verse and is taken up again in verse 14a, when, upon returning to the tomb, she sees Jesus and does not recognize him.

As for Luke, "the paschal narratives in chapter 24 of his gospel appear to be strongly organized around Peter and the Eleven. They are situated in Jerusalem rather than in Galilee and are focused on the universal mission of going forth from Jerusalem, empowered by the Holy Spirit, which is to be poured out on the day of Pentecost."[62]

Another text of fundamental importance in this context is that of 1 Corinthians 15, in which Paul transmits what he was taught concerning the death and Resurrection of Jesus, listing the names of those who saw the Risen One. Included in this list is a group of "more than five hundred brothers and sisters at one time, most of whom are still alive, though some have died" (1 Corinthians 15:6–7). The first letter to the Corinthians is dated at around 54–56 CE, a time very close to the Resurrection.

Death "for Our Sins"

Paul begins by stating that "Christ died for our sins." It is useless to pore over the details to discover who was responsible for it. As for the actual execution, the finger points to the Roman authorities and the imperial soldiers because, as subjects of the Roman government, the Jewish people did not have the power to impose the death penalty (John 18:31). The elders of Israel, the high priests and the scribes enter the picture as the ones who delivered Jesus to Pilate. However, it is obvious that the death of Jesus, who dies as an innocent victim for the sins of the world, is on a completely different level. *Every* human creature is responsible for his death, just as each human creature is included in the pardon that Jesus requests from the cross, because "they do not know what they are doing" (Luke 23:34).

As was noted in reference to the birth of Jesus, it is significant that both Jews and Gentiles are gathered around his cross. These two great families of humankind are both present at the crucifixion, reminding us that all people share in the responsibility for his death as well as the new life that will spring forth from it. Around the cross of Jesus are the Jews: Mary and John. There are also the Gentiles in their capacity as executors of the sentence, among whom are the centurion and the guards who realize: "Truly this man was God's Son" (Matthew 27:54). Also, the crowd that came to see the show and then went home beating their breasts (Luke 23:48) was composed of both Jews and Gentiles.[63]

Human Weakness

In the death and resurrection of Christ, an event of universal importance, there is again a particular contrast once pointed out by Micah in the prophecy regarding Bethlehem and now carried to the extreme. This contrast characterizes the entire narrative of the birth of Christ, because it stresses the coexistence of both the human and the divine within him. The humanity of Christ is manifested in his passion and death in all its weakness, "For he was crucified in weakness" (2 Corinthians 13:4); the deficiencies of the flesh are manifested in their ultimate consequence: death. Jesus assumes human nature along with all the weaknesses derived from sin, though he himself was without sin. But human nature is what it is, and Jesus takes it on as it is, except for those defects that are incompatible with the integrity of his person, human and divine.

Divine Power in the Resurrection

In the Resurrection, however, all the power of God is revealed: He "lives by the power of God" (2 Corinthians 13:4).

Death is not the end and must never be examined apart from resurrection. The death and Resurrection of Christ are two events which are strictly linked in time and cannot be separated from one another in terms of meaning or importance. The paschal mystery is an event of death and life, of life which comes from death: Jesus "died for all, so that those who live might live no longer for themselves, but for him who died and was raised for them" (2 Corinthians 5:15). At this point the constant theme found throughout the history of salvation—life coming forth even from difficult circumstances through the power of God—sounds its highest and most perfect note. This time life comes directly from death, its antithesis. The dawn of this truth, which shed its first rays of light at the time of Abraham, reaches high noon. Now the Christian can base his or her faith not only on a promise but on an event that has been realized.

The Resurrection is the completion of Christ's death, and death becomes a triumphant march toward the Father. Jesus accepts death in obedience to God's will, thus bringing his own will completely into line with that of the Father. He renounces all of the deep urges of his humanity in order to be at one with the divine will. In this way, death becomes the meritorious reason for the Resurrection. Christ's relinquishment of the demands of his humanity allows the divine power to take full possession of that humanity (Philippians 2:7); and divine power is life. Thus, Jesus rises from the dead. In the Resurrection the power of the Holy Spirit takes hold of the weakness of human flesh, permeating it with the life-giving breath of the Spirit, empowering it and transforming it.

Through the Work of the Holy Spirit

Just as at Nazareth Jesus was conceived in Mary's womb through the action of the Holy Spirit, so too the Holy Spirit is the author of the

Resurrection (Romans 8:11). The Father is the source of Resurrection as the first principle of all things; nevertheless, the person at work in the Resurrection—"the acting director"—is the Holy Spirit. All the earthly life of Jesus is compressed in a particular outpouring of the Spirit, from conception to Resurrection to Ascension.

From its beginning to its conclusion, the earthly life of Jesus is a progressive manifestation of the power of the Holy Spirit, sent from the Father and at work in the humanity of Christ. Jesus the human being is sanctified by the Holy Spirit at his conception and is glorified by the same Spirit at the moment of his Resurrection and Ascension. There is an earthly birth in Bethlehem in the weakness and lowliness of the human condition, and there is also a birth into the splendor of divine glory at Easter. Both events occur through the power of the Holy Spirit.

The prophets had spoken of a particular abundance of the Holy Spirit in the time of the Messiah (Joel 2:28). This age began on the day of Resurrection. It is a new kind of life that is offered to all men, women, and children, the first of whom is Christ (1 Corinthians 15:20–23).

The Humanity of Christ in the Glory of the Father

Jesus' Resurrection is not a matter of merely resuming the same life he had before his death, as in the case of Lazarus. Upon taking his physical body up again, Jesus returns to a new life; in his humanity he once again takes on the glory he had with the Father before the world began (John 17:4–5). He does not return to his condition before the Resurrection, or even to that of the Incarnation; rather, he recaptures his glory as Son of the Father, but this time in his humanity. The humanity of Jesus, wholly permeated with the Holy Spirit, now becomes the meekest and most intelligent instrument of divinity. In Christ's glorified humanity, sin has at last been totally conquered, because, in the words of Vagaggini, until Christ's Resurrection, "inasmuch as the Word was incarnated in a humbled state, not a glorious one, and, even more so, in a state of mortality, victory over sin had not yet been fully realized, not even in the person of Christ."[64]

Resurrection Is a Unifying Event

The death and Resurrection of Jesus carries an inherent demand for universality and therefore for unification. Thus, it is not without reason that the sign through which they are realized is the cross. It stretches its arms outward, to the east and to the west; it stretches upward, toward heaven, and is anchored in the earth. Saint Paul observes how "God was pleased to reconcile to himself all things, whether on earth or in heaven, by making peace through the blood of his cross" (Colossians 1:20). Here Saint Paul presents the Resurrection in its cosmic dimension: It is an event through which not only human beings are reconciled to God, but the entire universe is reconciled to the Father in Christ the man. Christ's human body, which comes back to life, is mysteriously linked to all of nature; therefore, nature itself cannot avoid receiving from the Resurrection a new, life-giving sap. We have already seen how at the birth of Jesus the natural elements were stirred by the presence of the child of Bethlehem. Now, at the Resurrection, the fracture that Adam's sin caused in humankind and between humankind and nature—which had been created for him and against which he rebelled—is healed. The original harmony is re-established in Christ in such a way that Saint John Chrysostom can say, "In him the heavens are risen, and the earth is risen; in him the world is risen."[65]

The world would have remained fractured had the blood of Christ not erased the sin that caused a chasm at the center of the universe, between the higher and the lower creation, that is, in humankind. Placed in this central position of the universe, Christ bore this rupture within himself during his earthly life, due to his existence in the flesh. Yet, with his death and resurrection, he himself abolished this conflict, and, in rising above all things, he himself reunited all things that were separated. All beings have in Christ their center of gravity and their point of convergence. "He who descended is the same one who ascended far above all the heavens, so that he might fill all things" (Ephesians 4:10).[66]

All this has occurred in Christ as the firstfruit of the new creation. We live in the time of waiting for the firstfruit to bear its full fruit—when "God will be all in all" (1 Corinthians 15:28).

Chapter 51

The Gift of the Holy Spirit and Parousia

The Outpouring of the Spirit

The first fruit borne by Christ the "firstfruit" is Pentecost. The Holy Spirit, who permeated the human body of Jesus and brought him back to life, is by nature dynamic and diffusive. Indeed, after the Resurrection, Jesus has the power to pass it on to the apostles (John 20:22). He does this through his glorified humanity.

Through the Glorified Body of Christ

The glorified body of Christ becomes the effusive medium of the Spirit, and therefore of new life for human beings. The gift of the Holy Spirit received by Jesus in his humanity is communicated to whoever encounters him in his humanity. In fact, the greatest source of the Holy Spirit is the Eucharist.

The Holy Spirit communicates to every person some of the abundance of the gift Jesus received as a human being; it internalizes and individualizes in each person the salvation realized by Christ through his death and resurrection. However, the Spirit's action occurs through the Risen Christ. One must view the death, Resurrection, glorification, and sending forth of the Holy Spirit as one saving act of God. The earthly mission of Jesus, having begun with the action of the Spirit at his conception, is concluded in the sharing of this same Spirit with all human beings. At Pentecost, the Spirit, who is salvation and who first resides in the person of Jesus, begins to be diffused by descending upon the Virgin and an initial small group of Christians (Acts 2:1ff.). They are the first seed of the Church, the society that lives the very life of Christ, so much so that they are considered to be his own Body.

And, Therefore, through the Sacraments

The gift of the Holy Spirit must permeate the world more and more until the day when "God will be all in all." The Church was born as a small seed and is destined to develop as the mustard seed develops. It develops gradually throughout time, in every human creature who comes in contact with Christ through the sacraments, especially the Eucharist, and in daily life. In this way, Christians come to partake in the gift of the Holy Spirit. Easter, the sacrifice of Christ for the glory of the Father, and Pentecost, the outpouring of the Holy Spirit that brings the salvation won by Christ through the will of the Father, continue in each Christian.

The Hope of the People of God: Parousia

Thus, the history continues straining toward a hope: the salvation of all people and the expansion of the covenant to the "ends of the earth," when the saved person will carry with him or her the entire universe, which "has been groaning in labor pains until now" (Romans 8:22). Indeed, the redemption of the universe is connected to human redemption. Just as the earth was cursed because of humankind's sin, so, too, it will be restored and redeemed by the influence—positive this time— that redeemed human beings exercise upon it.[67] Thus, all things will be recapitulated in Christ, who will reinstate the kingdom of God, and his kingdom will have no end.

It is toward this expectation and hope that the believer stretches even today. The Christian believer bases his or her hope upon an event which has already been realized; the Jewish believer bases hope on the promise of such an event. In this expectation and hope, Christians and Jews cannot but rediscover one another, because they both fix their gaze on the same point of the horizon: the Messiah who will come or will return in glory.

Notes

1 "Towards Christian Unity," n. 140. This theme is taken up again in "Note Regarding the Correct Presentation of the Jews and Judaism," 1985, n. 10.

2 E. Schillebeeckx, *Marie, Mere de la redemption* (Ed. du Cerf, 1962).

3 *Dei verbum,* 2.

4 *Genesis Homilies,* 10:3.

5 *Hom. II in Ps. 38, PG 12, 1403, 8.*

6 *Enarr. 25 in Ps. 38,* PL 14, 1051, C.

7 *De Catechizandis Rudibus,* 6, 6.

8 H. Renckens, *Prehistory and the History of Salvation* (Pauline Editions, 1962).

9 Tertullian, *De Baptismo,* 3: 2ff.

10 In paeleo-Christian art, the fish is the symbol of Christ and the Christians.

11 H. Renkins, *Prehistory and the History of Salvation* (Pauline Editions, 1962).

12 The tree of life is associated with the tree of knowledge, because life and knowledge are two indivisible goods. Life is given to us in order for us to obtain knowledge or consciousness. Without consciousness, there is no real life. This concept is clarified in John 17:3: "And this is eternal life: that they may know you, the only true God, and Jesus Christ whom you have sent."

13 The child whose name is Immanuel (God with us) and who will eat curds and honey until "he knows how to refuse the evil and choose the good" (Isaiah 7:14, 15) has been traditionally understood as an antithetical allusion to Adam, who eats the forbidden fruit instead of the paradisiacal food of curds and honey, thus refusing good and choosing evil.

14 See Luke 4:1ff. The first temptation of Jesus deals with eating: "He ate nothing at all during those days, and when they were over he was famished. The devil said to him, 'If you are the Son of God, command this stone to turn into a loaf of bread.'" In Genesis the temptation is also expressed in terms of eating: "But God said, 'You shall not eat of the tree in the middle of the garden.'" The second assault on the Lord follows immediately with a temptation to self-elevation: "To you I will give their glory and all this authority . . . [i]f you, then, will worship me, it will all be yours." In the same way Satan had said to Adam and Eve: "God knows that when you eat [the fruit] your eyes will be opened and you will be like God." In the last temptation the devil wants to place a doubt in Jesus' mind: "*If* you are the Son of God, throw

yourself down from here." Satan had also placed a doubt in Eve's mind: "You will *not* die . . ."

15 *Adv. Haer.,* 5, 23, PL 1185.

16 *De Carne Christi,* PL II, 7822b.

17 PL II, 782.

18 Cyril of Jerusalem, PG 33, 981, A.

19 *Dialogue with Trypho,* 138:2, 3.

20 *De Baptismo,* 8:3

21 BCE ("before the common era") and CE ("of the common era") denote the same periods of time as bc ("before Christ") and AD (*Anno Domini,* "in the year of our Lord"), respectively, and are conventionally used in biblical scholarship.

22 S. Lyonnet, *Dieci meditazioni su San Paolo* (Paidera, 1966), pages 9–24.

23 *Baptismal Catechesis,* 5.

24 Ibid.

25　PL 12, 203ff.

26 N. Lohfink, *L'Alleanza mai revocata* (*The Unbreakable Covenant*). Brescia, 1991.

27 *De Sacramentis,* 4:12.

28 PG 33, 1068.

29 *Dem.* 12:8; PS I, 521.

30 *De Baptismo,* 9:1.

31 *De Mysterium,* 3:12.

32 *De Baptismo,* 9.

33 PG 80, 257.

34 *Treatise on the Holy Spirit,* PG 32, 121.

35 Scholars argue over which passages can truly be considered the songs of the suffering servant of the Lord and over their actual length.

36 M. Remaud, *Chretiens devant Israel serviteur de Dieu* (Paris: Cerf, l983).

37 A fundamental text on Jewish–Christian relations is the Second Vatican Council *Declaration on the Relation of the Church to Non-Christian Religions* (*Nostra Aetate* (1965): n. 4), in relation to which other documents have followed, such as *Guidelines and Suggestions for Implementing the Conciliar Declaration "Nostra Aetate,"* 1975 (*Orientazioni e suggerimenti);* Notes on the Correct Way to Present the Jews and Judaism, 1985 (*Note per una corretta presentazione degli ebrei e dell'ebraismo*). See also L. Sestieri and G. Cereti, *Le chiese cristiane e l'ebraismo, raccolta di testi 1947-82* (Genoa 1983); AAVV. *Secundo le Scritture. Chiese Cristiane e popolo di Dio,* edited by G. Bottoni, L. Nason (Bologna, 2002). In particular, see C. Stephan Ragazzi, *Ebrai e cristiani negli anni della*

svolta (1947–1985), and *Il dialogo cristiano ebraico: una rassegna di documenti delle chiese dal 1986-2000*. Of a didactic character, S. Cavalletti, *La storia da Abramo alla parusia* (Saveria Mannelli, 2004): timeline of history and two accompanying booklets. (Note: this work has been translated into English as *Remember the Lord Your God: A History of the Jewish People* [Liturgy Training Publications: 2004].)

38 E. Schillebeeckx, *Cristo sacramento dell' incontro con Dio* (Ed. Paoline, 1962), page 32.

39 C. Vagaggini, *Caro salutis est cardo, corporeita eucaristica e liturgica* (Desclee, Roma 1966), pages 122, 131.

40 Ibid.

41 R. Guardini, *La Mere du Seigneur* (Paris, 1961), page 44.

42 PL 38, 1074.

43 Ibid.

44 S. Cipriani, "Maria, membro eletto della Chiesa," in *Via, Verita e Vita,* page 13ff.

45 S. Lyonnet, Le recit de l'Annonciation e la maternite divine de la Sainte Vierge (Rome, 1956).

46 K. Rahner, *Maria, Madre del Signore* (Fossano, 1960), page 16.

47 PL 11, 7822.

48 K. Rahner, op. cit., page 37.

49 *The Anchor Bible,* New York, 1971.

50 For example, Suetonius, *The Life of Caesar,* page 81.

51 A classic intertestamental book is Emil Shurer, *A History of the Jewish People in the Time of Jesus Christ* (T & T Clark, Edinburgh, 1890).

52 S. Cavalletti, *Judaism and Christian Spirituality* (Rome: Studium, 1966).

53 Cf. L. Levine. *The Synagogue in Late Antiquity* (Philadelphia: The American Schools of Oriental Research, 1987).

54 For these comparisons I refer to A. Guilding's "The Fourth Gospel and Jewish Worship in the Fourth Gospel," *Journal of Biblical Literature,* 1962: 329ff.

55 *Vatican Council II: The Conciliar and Post Conciliar Documents.* Ed. Austin Flannery, O.P. New York: Costello Publishing Company, 1975. 1: n2.

56 Catechism of the Catholic Church, n. 1061, 1116

57 Ibid. n.1116.

58 A. Ammassari, *La resurrezione nell'insegnamento, nella profezia, nelle apparizione di Gesu* (Citta Nuova Editrice, Volumes I and II, 1976).

59 Regarding this expression, see the chapter 43 in this book.

60 Ammassari, page 128

61 S. G. F. Brandon, "Christ in Verbal and Depicted Imagery," in *Christianity, Judaism and Other Greco-Roman Cults,* Part II, ed. by J. Neusner (Leiden, 1975), pages 164–172.

62 Ammassari, page 197.

63 See the Declaration on the Relation of the Church to Non-Christian Religions *Nostra aetate,* 4, and the comment of B. Hussar, *Elle Dici* (Torino, 1966), page 223.

64 Cyprian Vagaggine, osb, *The Flesh, Instrument of Salvation* (Staten Island: Alba House, 1969).

65 PL 16:404.

66 Durwell, *The Resurrection of Jesus, the Mystery of Salvation* (Ed. Paoline, 1962).

67 S. Lyonnet, *La storia della salvezza nella Lettera ai Romani* (Napoli, 1966), page 221ff.

Catechesis of
the Good Shepherd
Publications

Catechesis of the Good Shepherd Publications is an imprint of Liturgy Training Publications (LTP). Further information about these publications is available from LTP or from The Catechesis of the Good Shepherd, P.O. Box 1084, Oak Park IL 60304; http://www.cgsusa.org/. Requests for information about other aspects of the Catechesis also should be directed to this address.

CATECHESIS OF THE GOOD SHEPHERD IMPRINT:
Additional Works by Sofia Cavalletti

The Religious Potential of the Child: Experiencing Scripture and Liturgy with Young Children

The Religious Potential of the Child, 6 to 12 Years Old

The Good Shepherd and the Child: A Joyful Journey

Living Liturgy: Elementary Reflections (The History of the Kingdom of God Part 2: Liturgy in the Building of the Kingdom (forthcoming))

Ways to Nurture the Relationship with God

Way of Holy Joy: Selected Writings of Sofia Cavalletti (2012)

Catechesis of the Good Shepherd: Essential Realities (a collection of essays celebrating 50 years of the Catechesis of the Good Shepherd)

Discovering the Real Spiritual Life of Children (video)